A Private Developer's Roadmap for

AFFORDABLE HOUSING

Profitable Rental Apartment Solutions in Canada

Other Books by Derek Lobo

The Future Apartment Developer: The Blueprint for Building Rental Apartments and Intergenerational Wealth (MPS-Dala, 2021)

A *Field Guide to Rental Apartment Development by the Numbers: Building and Testing a Detailed Financial Feasibility Model* (MPS-Dala, 2021)

The Feasibility Study Determines the Apartment You Build: How to Build the Right Apartment Building in the Right Location for the Right Resident (MPS-Dala, 2021)

Finding Money to Build Apartments: Make Better Deals by Finding Cheaper Capital (MPS-Dala, 2021)

A Field Guide to Municipal Taxes and Operating Costs: Decreasing Your Operating Costs to Maximize Value (MPS-Dala, 2021)

The Four Factors That Drive Rent: Why $100 More in Rent = $24,000 in Increased Value (MPS-Dala, 2021)

Intensifying Existing Developments with Apartments: Apartments Are the Most Profitable Additions When Intensifying Land (MPS-Dala, 2021)

Building Apartments With a Joint Venture Partner: Structuring a Deal so That the Lender, Developer, and Partner Win (MPS-Dala, 2021)

Writing and Executing the Marketing Plan: Strategies to Get Your Building Full at the Highest Rent (MPS-Dala, 2021)

Writing and Executing a Sales and Leasing Plan: Hiring, Training, Managing, and Compensating Your Leasing Staff for Maximum Results (MPS-Dala, 2021)

Designing Apartments for the Future: Meeting Modern Expectations With Innovative Design (MPS-Dala, 2021)

Becoming a Successful Merchant Apartment Builder: Developing a Business Plan and Growing Your Wealth (MPS-Dala, 2021)

Finding and Acquiring Land for Apartment Development: Processes for Site Selection Through Closing (MPS-Dala, 2021)

The Intentional Apartment Developer: A Programmatic Guide for Planning, Designing, Building, Leasing, Managing and Selling (Dala, 2022)

A Private Developer's Roadmap for

AFFORDABLE HOUSING

Profitable Rental Apartment Solutions in Canada

APARTMENT University

DEREK LOBO

DALA™
Derek A. Lobo & Associates
Group of Companies

A Private Developer's Roadmap for Affordable Housing:
Profitable Rental Apartment Solutions in Canada

Derek Lobo, Apartment University

Published by DALA Inc.

Derek Lobo
Apartment University
905-331-5700
derek@derek-lobo.com
derek.lobo@rockadvisorsinc.com
RockAdvisorsInc.com

ISBN: 978-1-7773648-6-1

Printed in Canada
First Edition, June 2022

Editor: Rory d'Eon
Contributing Editor: Natan Ary
Proofreading: Geri Savits-Fine
Interior Layout: Adam Carter
Cover: Adam Carter
Project Management: Rod Schulhauser & DALA Inc.

Dedication

I dedicate this book to all the courageous men and women who put it all on the line to build rental apartments.

These people are my heroes!

DEREK
LOBO

Table Of Contents

List of Figures

Acknowledgements

There has never been a more important time to get a project like this into the hands of apartment developers. It took time to bring together industry experts and craft a message that would directly impact the housing crisis and make affordable housing projects more enticing to the developer.

I would like to thank Natan Ary, Ismail Ibrahim, Mark Kay, Noor Khan, and Graeme Stewart for their insight and expertise. Our Rock Advisors team also played in important role in executing the webinars, in addition to the creation of this book. I am blessed with a great team who pull together content, expertise, knowledge, relationships, and skills to make my vision a reality.

I am thankful for all our clients and collaborators! I also need to continually extend my appreciation to Dan Sullivan, whose mentorship and friendship have been pivotal in shaping my strategic thinking and opening new avenues for me to explore both at work and at home.

Thank you all!

A Message from Derek Lobo

The documentary *Shelter: An immigrant story that helped shape a city*, is a chronicle of the immigrants who came to Canada in the '40s and '50s, many of them Holocaust survivors. Some of them went on to build half a million apartments in the city of Toronto during the '60s and '70s. This group of people, probably no more than 20 in all, organized fundraising events and created partnerships to build these apartments. Their example shows us what simple, good government policy and a conscientious private sector can do together.

Had these apartments not been built, I don't believe Toronto would be the city it is today. Just think of all the new Canadians who found attainable housing and proceeded to build themselves a commendable life.

Like many of you, I'm also an immigrant. Originally from Pakistan, my family—my parents and five children—came to Canada in 1966 when I was only eight years old. Surviving only on my father's meagre income, we were fortunate enough to find a decent place to live in the Jane-Finch area of Toronto.

That modest beginning gave us a solid foundation upon which to begin our lives in Canada. The reason I say this is because the first four or five years in a child's development are crucial to their continuing success as contributing members of society.

Coming into a new country, as we did, was a rebirth in many ways. We came to Canada for economic reasons. However, this country was far different from the one we came from. As kids, having the stability our parents provided gave us all the time and nurturing needed to familiarize ourselves with, and understand, this new culture.

I think I knew it back then, but only on a subconscious level. As my working life progressed, the idea of being able to afford our first home was one of the key reasons we became productive Canadians.

However, that first home didn't materialize out of nowhere. Someone with vision and a keen sense of purpose built that home knowing they were providing an essential component of society's well-being. I believe my family is a personal testament to that.

It's interesting that I moved into one of those immigrant-built buildings. I joke and say, "I read my first lease when I was eight." That's because I helped my parents sublet it.

Of even greater interest, when I began working, it was for those same developers—who were then in their 60s—the ones that built the actual unit we lived in. It's no wonder I see myself as being born for this business.

Working in the private sector, I know that profit is essential. But I also know that having purpose is essential as well. My business experience has taught me that building attainable housing can be both profitable and fulfilling.

So, if you get off to a good start paying 30% or 40% of your income on good housing for you and your family, you're going to settle into life well. I believe solid grounding makes you a better and more productive Canadian.

On the Business Side

As a business person, it is my view that your return on equity from affordable housing can be greater than building conventional apartments for these reasons: 1) the sources of funds are more leveraged (i.e., lower equity percentage); 2) loan terms are more favourable; 3) lease-up is faster; and 4) the vacancy rate is lower, providing you go through the steps needed.

However, there's more work to do here. If we build enough attainable housing, we think many Canadians would have an easier start, and ultimately be more successful, pay more taxes, and contribute immensely to society in general.

Many of the housing built 30 years ago has now become attainable housing. But we're not building enough units today to satisfy the current demand, let alone the demand in 30 years. It's my view that attainable housing can only be addressed by an accelerated supply, which can only be delivered by the private market and coordinated governmental programs that simplify and streamline the process.

On the Word "Affordable"

I'm not sold on the word "affordable." It makes me think about metro housing from the '60s, '70s and '80s. This is not what's being discussed within this book.

A better description would be "workforce housing." This would be designed for working-class people with working-class jobs and incomes who are in the middle or the median range of Canadians—in essence, just regular people, but with a more limited disposable income than homeowners.

Introduction

By 2030 everyone in Canada will have a home that they can afford and meets their needs.
- CMHC

The affordable housing market is emerging as an exciting new opportunity for developers, and this is extraordinary for the housing industry. This market promises to quickly become an asset class onto itself. Two factors have come together to make this happen: political will and society's desire for environmental, social, and governance (ESG) responsibility.

The advantage will go to those developers, consultants, brokers, and architects who quickly realize the benefits of working with affordable housing. Those willing to invest time and resources to become programmatically organized can realize the potential profits of this new, and viable, asset class.

As with all emerging opportunities, there are both certainties and uncertainties. The certainties are:

- Strong and continuous demand
- Better financing terms are available
- Pressure on developers, institutions, and government to be socially conscious

Affordable housing fits into these certainties exceptionally well. The key is to generate some liquidity into this market beyond the current municipality-owned nonprofits and into a market where the private sector builds the housing, and the institutions buy and manage them.

The uncertainties are:

- Information is scattered
- The exit strategy
- Exit cap rates
- Education for institutional buyers
- Widespread decisions by municipalities to waive fees to improve the feasibility of private affordable housing initiatives

However, the availability of a learning portal (such as ours), where all pertinent information is readily available and well organized, will allow all stakeholders to always be on the same page. With all government programs detailed, interactions well documented, and sample financial scenarios available, it's far easier for interested parties to take advantage of this growing asset class. And with enough affordable housing being built, exit strategies will become clearer.

Knowing that finding tenants to fill the units is not an issue, buyers will become available. Affordable rental cap rates are equal to or lower than conventional rental market cap rates. However, the stability of tenant availability will help make investments profitable.

Institutional investors may be interested if they are brought into the picture once sources of funds for affordable rental projects are confirmed, or in place—the affordable rental investment then becomes very appealing. It's vital that developers beginning affordable housing projects become fluent with available programs and how they interact, and also understand that there is a viable financial opportunity in this asset class.

What you'll gain over the next five chapters is an early knowledge of the ins and outs of affordable housing for first-move advantage and an awareness that this is a long-term process that can be navigated successfully.

We'll cover:

1. Why developers should consider pivoting to affordable housing
2. Where and what to build
3. Government grants and financing for affordable housing
4. Working with municipalities and stakeholders
5. Developing a business plan to build affordable housing

The affordable market dilemma took years to create and will take just as long to solve. Still, we think governments are now open to developing policies that work for all stakeholders—allowing these policies and private capital to work together to develop an affordable rental housing boom, as was the case in the 1960s and '70s.

Though this is not a new idea, it's one that needs a concerted effort so developers can work within clear guidelines, enabling them to expand this asset class so it can grow quickly and continue in the longer term. This asset class will then fulfil the overdue affordable housing needs in Canada.

1

Why Build Affordable Housing?

Introduction

Why would a developer want to enter the affordable housing market?

First and foremost, there is an urgent need. The shift away from affordable housing that began in the 1970s, along with the changes in the housing market in general, has left an unfilled gap resulting in many individuals and families unable to find decent affordable housing.

Secondly, we think that once the affordable market gets going, there will be sustainable market liquidity. This is important because you can only develop an asset class once there are buyers, sellers, and support from the trades, consultants, and ancillary services.

Thirdly, with a stable supply of renters, the affordable housing fundamentals are stable and recession proof. There is an exceptional debt environment, in general, with funds available for affordable housing featuring lower rates, and longer terms and amortization periods.

With these fundamentals in place, there is an opportunity for merchant developers to build wealth and a portfolio of long-term stable assets for their family and for generations down the road.

Our company has made a commitment to enter this asset class because it's an important investment in the growth of Canadian housing. We see a programmatic opportunity to build affordable apartments where the stability is extraordinarily high, and the returns are likely better than expected. We believe that as a company and as an industry we should all turn our attention to affordable housing.

Risk During a Recession

Of all the asset classes in the industry, affordable housing has been affected the least.

LOWEST RISK

- **Affordable Housing**
- **Self Storage**
- **Industrial**
- **Apartments**
- **Student Housing** (unknown)
- **Office** (medium- to long-term risk)
- **Retail** (short-, medium-, and long-term risk)
- **Hotels/Hospitality** (severe short-term risk)

HIGHEST RISK

Figure 1.1 - Asset Risk by Class

We feel the affordable housing class gives the economy and industry stability. However, developers must also have bandwidth and see a future in that market.

The onus on all levels of government is to get together and streamline the process. The 2021 political platforms from Canada's two largest political parties emphasized the need for this to happen. The private sector must then respond by designing and building affordable housing. However, there are challenges that must be overcome.

Is Affordable Housing a Human Right?

Canada's main political parties believe affordable housing is a human right. In his speeches, Prime Minister Trudeau has said so. Once housing is formally designated a human right, its definition and surrounding obligations change.

Figure 1.2 - Is Housing a Right?

The UN also considers housing a right. It has reported that the responsibility of housing is the responsibility of the state. If the state is supposed to provide housing, a nation becomes responsible to house its people.

Environmental, Social, and Governance (ESG)

ESG is an umbrella concept guiding businesses.

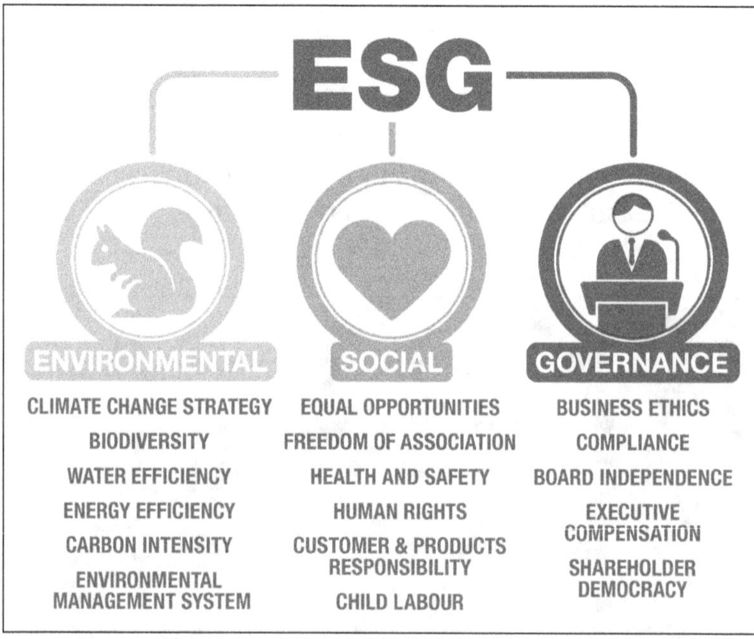

Figure 1.3 - ESG

Though many institutions, public companies, and governments are actively talking about ESG, there is a significant cost to implementing its principles.

Affordable housing fits well into ESG's purview. In our opinion, there's going to be a lot more effort put into building social and affordable housing for low- and middle-income earners in Canada. This is an excellent opportunity for developers and all those that support this industry.

The Current Situation

The current situation and housing environment in the US is not the same as in Canada. The affordable market is well established in the US. In Canada, it is not. For a variety of reasons, Canada must create its own solution to its affordable housing crisis. We feel that, under the current government programs, we are creating our own long-term solution.

The United States

In the US, there are two types of affordable housing: Section 8 and Section 42 Housing. What's important is that affordable housing trades. Once it trades, it results in liquidity.

	SECTION 42	SECTION 8 VOUCHERS
Administrated by	State Housing Credit Agency	Federal (HUD)
Maximum family income	60% of area median income	50% of area median income
Minimum family income	0% of area median income	0% of area median income
Rent restriction	30% of area median income	Market rent
Lock-in Period	30 years	N/A
Profit realized from	Development process	Operation process
Ability to generate NOI	Limited	Strong
Investment return	Fixed at inception	Varies with market situation

Figure 1.4 - Affordable Housing in the US

There's a fraternity of people who work in the affordable housing sector: developers, consultants, lawyers, buyers, and brokers. A developer can build, make a decent profit, then have someone buy the project as a core holding for themselves, or it can be put into a fund or a public company.

Canada

This type of active and sustainable market may soon develop in Canada. But as of now, the transactions related to affordable housing have been few.

Over the last 20 years of transactions, the phrase affordable housing was mentioned in the building description only 40 times. Only 20% of those 40 were between private sector buyers or sellers. All the rest were from nonprofit to nonprofit. However, we think that is going to change.

Getting ahead of that trend can be a significant business opportunity for developers. We sense that we're on the cusp of this change. Our business case is that we predict there will be much more affordable housing built, funded, and, if set up properly, transacted.

Liquidity Is Key

The key to affordable housing, and a unique problem for Canada, is liquidity. In the United States, affordable housing can be built knowing a group of buyers is available. Those buyers then purchase the development and allow developers to move on to the next project, as done in the commercial market.

Without liquidity we don't think we're going to see a lot of affordable housing built because developing apartments is a cash intensive business. Developers need to, and want to, keep their money active.

Example One: Liquidity

This is an example of liquidity and how it is changing in the apartment sector.

If a developer builds 100 units in Toronto, Vancouver, Calgary, or Montreal, they're going to get a fair number (10 to 15) of buyers for that project if they lease it up. But if they build that same project in a smaller market like Peterborough, Stratford, or North Battleford, Saskatchewan, they will attract fewer buyers. Therefore, the price for the same type of building is going to be less in those smaller centres. Additionally, the cap rate is going to be higher because there is less liquidity. So, with liquidity comes cap rate compression and price increase.

To enable affordable housing to flourish, we will have to create a policy where affordable housing can be built by developers, then owned by the private sector and institutions while remaining affordable. That liquidity will allow cap rates to go down because there will be more buyers at the table.

The point we are making is that, in this last economic downturn, we've seen some groups afraid to invest in high-end buildings located in the downtown core. The same groups are now buying in secondary and tertiary markets, bringing liquidity to those smaller centres. As a result, we'll see more cap rate compression as more buyers come to the market.

If we can create liquidity in the affordable housing sector, there's going to be much more money available and a lot more affordable housing built.

Example Two: Student Housing

We have been involved in Canadian student housing from the very beginning. We've conducted seminars, consulted, and completed brokerage. At first, there were very few buyers. But as the buyers increased, the cap rate compressed.

Student housing is still a secondary- and tertiary-type business; it's not a primary business in Canada yet, but as of late, there have been some positive signs. The gist of it is, if enough product is built, the buyers will be there.

The problem we encountered with student housing is this: pension funds were not interested in buying only one or two student housing assets—they wanted to see a market like that of Europe and the US where there were many assets to choose from. In essence, it was a chicken-and-egg situation, with developers saying, "Is there a buyer?" and buyers saying, "Are there enough developers?"

However, we believe that with smart policy changes and good financing, liquidity can be brought to the affordable housing sector.

Example Three: Rethinking the Market

Dream REIT has created the Dream Impact Trust for affordable housing. We have completed several studies for this company. They partnered with private developers to build a large redevelopment deal in Toronto's West Donlands.

The client was bound by specific development agreements. Therefore, in the feasibility study, we had to rethink this market in terms of unit sizing, amenity provisions, parking, and market rents versus affordable rents.

Incentives

Incentives at the time of writing:

City of Toronto

1. Open Door
2. CreateTO Housing Now

Provincial

3. Home for Good Program
4. Affordable Housing Lands Program

Federal

5. National Housing Strategy (NHS)
6. National Housing Co-Investment Initiative Fund
7. Rental Construction Financing Initiative (RCFi)
8. CMHC Co-Investment Fund
9. MLI Affordable Flex
10. MLI Market Rental Construction
11. CMHC Incentives: Predevelopment Seed Grants and Loans
12. Other: FCM/grant support for sustainable housing and energy efficiency

Joint Provincial-Federal

13. Canada-Ontario Housing Benefit (COHB) Program
14. Investment in Affordable Housing for Ontario Program

Becoming Business as Usual

Building affordable housing is only going to be successful if it scales to the private sector. How do we unlock the huge amount of land assets we have throughout the region and throughout Canada? Much of this relates to deep retrofits, resilient housing, and complete community redesigns.

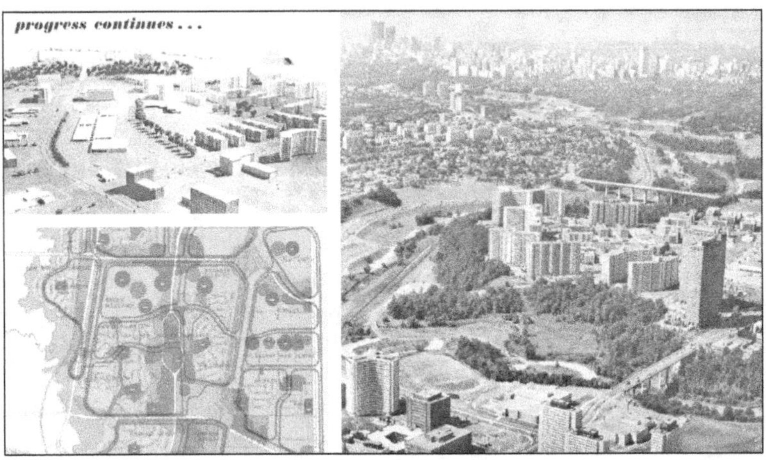

Figure 1.5 - Affordable Housing Retrofits

The older apartment boom of this country rivalled any similar apartment boom on the continent, resulting in significantly more multi-residential units built per capita than in the US during this period. At that time, Canada got the policy mixture right to create an enormous private-sector-led housing boom.

Three Key Factors

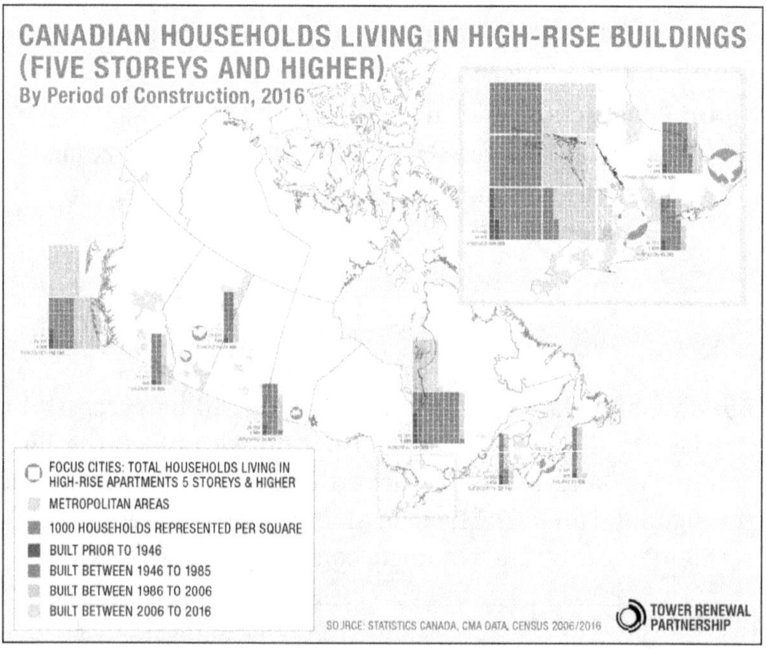

Figure 1.6 - Canadians Living in High-rises

We had regulations stating Canada needs this housing everywhere in terms of: 1) economic policy; 2) favourable taxation from the federal and provincial governments; and 3) a development industry ready to meet demands of a quickly growing country. More than half of all existing high-rises across the country were built before 1980. These still form the bulk of what currently exists.

Figure 1.7 - Retrofit Development

Development stopped in the early 1980s due to many factors. One factor was a tax change that made building unfavourable. As a result, Cadillac Fairview omitted entire portfolios, stating it no longer made economic sense. However, that tax change can be reversed to make affordable housing attractive once more.

Figure 1.8 - Tower Renewal Advisory Network

The Tower Renewal Partnership has many partners focused on optimizing our housing resources—particularly opportunities for more affordable housing development.

> *By 2030 everyone in Canada will have a home that they can afford and meets their needs.*
> *- CMHC*

This is a radical statement—and we have just a very few years left to meet this goal. This drive has led to billions of dollars on the table from different departments of the federal government, CMHC, Canadian Infrastructure Bank, and others. More funds are also on the way as comparable provincial programs. This is money that stakeholders can use to find ways of making development projects more palatable.

Housing Rehabilitation

From the preservation and retrofit space, the figure below shows a recent project turning an older apartment into a net-zero building. It shows the level of government commitments needed to make this happen.

Figure 1.9 - Older Apartment Retrofit Into a Net-Zero Building

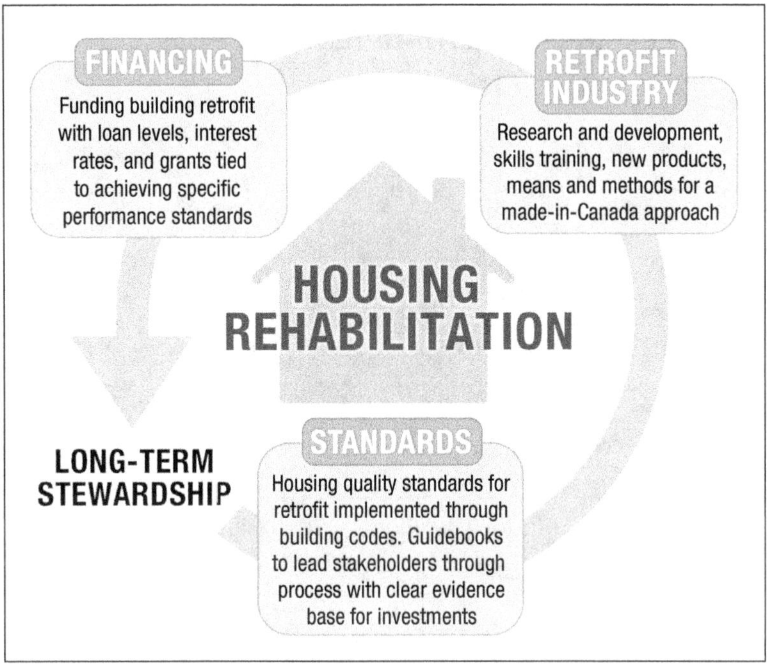

Figure 1.10 - The Financial Environment

This is really about the right financial environment, building to specific standards, and making sure that we have industry readiness to bring workers to the table.

We think we know that there are certain indicators showing the market is changing in some spaces—there's an endless supply of opportunities and endless renter demand. This is an important change.

Case Study: Surplus Land

One area of focus is surplus land. For an owner of an asset with surplus land, significant opportunity exists.

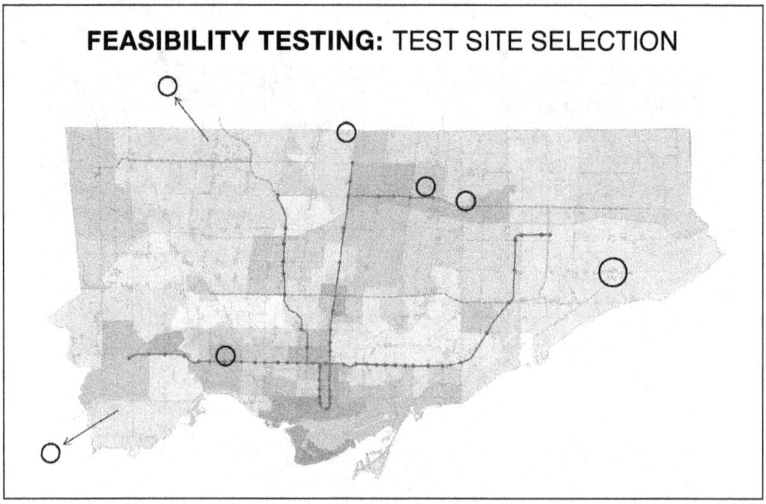

Figure 1.11 - Finding Test Sites

Astoundingly, there is more than 2,000 hectares of surplus land associated with older buildings that can be developed within the Greater Toronto Area (GTA) alone. These surplus lands are prime for affordable rentals as demand in these locations has been proven and they are in heavily populated areas. A block-planning study can be completed at the outset to maximize the potential density of the surplus land.

The following pages show an analysis we performed for the province examining best practices to make this happen.

Figure 1.12a - Spaces Available to Retrofit

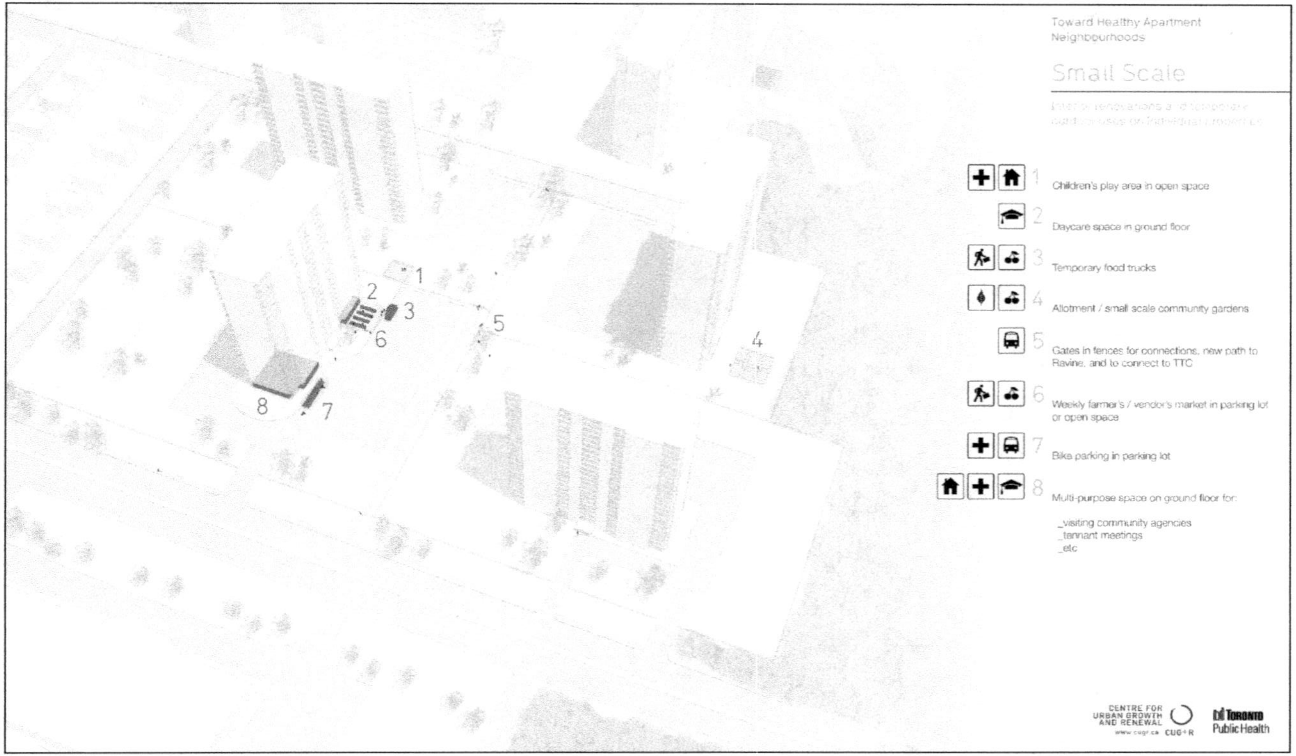

Figure 1.12b - Spaces Available to Retrofit

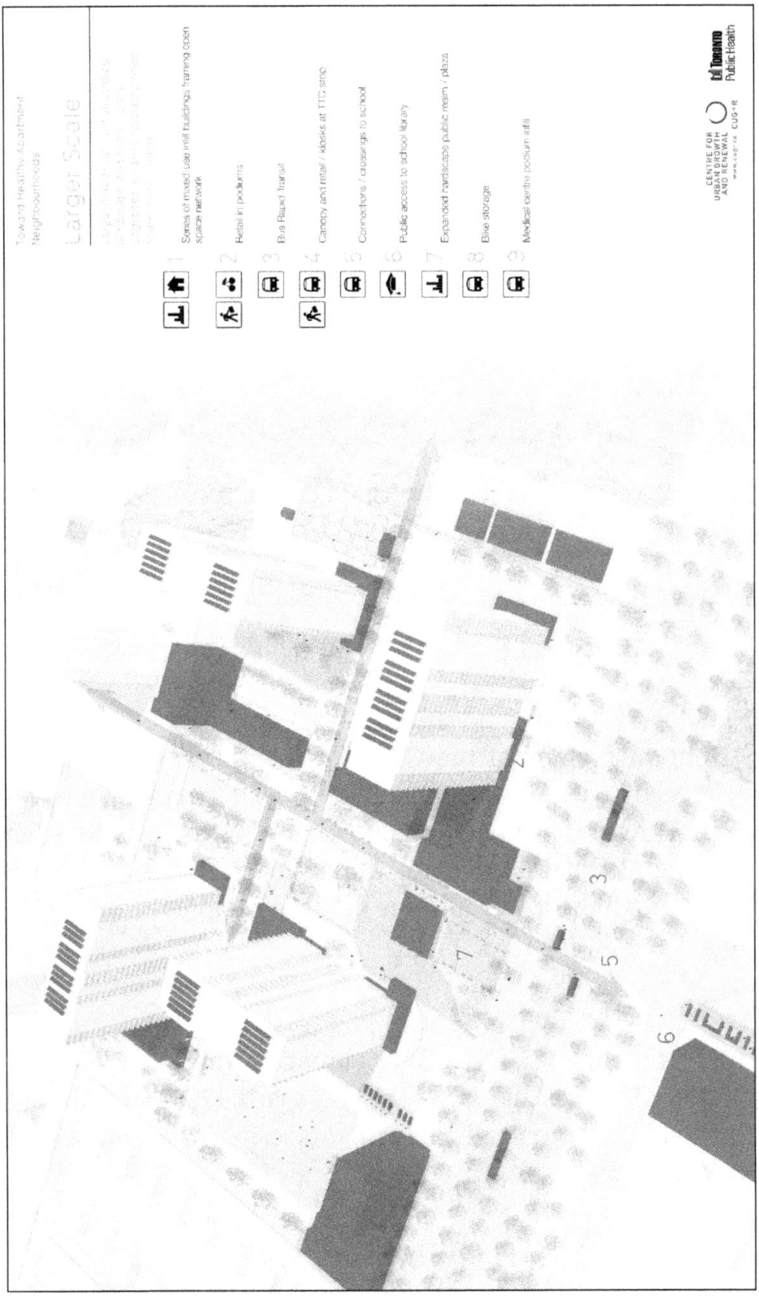

Figure 1.12c - Spaces Available to Retrofit

There are many examples from the UK and elsewhere—one is shown below. In effect, when the policy alignment is right, there are many places to build beyond those stuck in the centre.

Figure 1.13 - A European Example of a Retrofit

Outside of central locations, such as Peterborough or peripheral regions of the GTA, or other large cities, there's more resilience for affordable rentals because land values are lower. However, rental rates are also lower. Risk is reduced by bringing affordability versus the absorption rate for luxury (which might be lower in some of these peripheral zones).

Case Study

The following case study compares three projects: a project with 100% condo, one with a mix (70/30) of market/affordable that met all the program criteria, and one with 100% affordable rental.

Private Sector Results (Per Square Foot Buildable)

Financial Testing Summary – Private Sector, 30% Affordable (@80%AMR) + 70% Market Condominium

Strong Market	100% Market Condo (Benchmark)	No Incentives + Full PLG Process		Pre-Zoned + No Incentives		Open Door + Full Planning Process		Open Door + Pre-Zoned		Federal Grants (15% Cost, $100 psf) Only		Federal Grants (15% Cost, $90 psf) and Municipal Incentive	
	Commercial Loan	Commercial Loan	CMHC Loan	Commercial Loan	CMHC Loan	Commercial Loan	CMHC Loan	Commercial Loan	CMHC Loan	Commercial Loan	CMHC Loan	Commercial Loan	CMHC Loan
Total Cost (Soft + Hard)	$740	$670	$660	$620	$610	$640	$630	$600	$590	$670	$660	$600	$590
Hard Costs	$380	$370	$370	$350	$350	$370	$370	$350	$350	$370	$370	$350	$350
Soft Costs	$360	$290	$280	$270	$260	$270	$260	$250	$240	$290	$280	$250	$240
Developer Equity Investment Required	$180	$170	$160	$150	$150	$160	$160	$150	$150	$170	$160	$150	$150
Are Land Value and Purchaser Deposits Sufficient to Cover Equity Required?	yes	yes	yes	yes	yes	yes	yes	yes	yes	yes	yes	yes	yes
Total Revenue	$1,240	$1,000	$1,000	$950	$950	$1,000	$1,000	$950	$950	$1,100	$1,090	$1,040	$1,040
Revenue Received at Project Completion (Condos) Before Disposal of Rental	$1,240	$1,240	$1,230	$1,170	$1,170	$1,240	$1,230	$1,170	$1,170	$1,380	$1,370	$1,300	$1,290
Proceeds from Rental Component Disposal	$0	$450	$450	$440	$440	$450	$450	$440	$440	$450	$450	$440	$440
Measures of Performance													
Total developer return after paying off all costs (no land cost*) - PV	***$350***	***$240***	***$240***	***$260***	***$260***	***$250***	***$260***	***$270***	***$280***	***$310***	***$310***	***$340***	***$350***
% Reduction from Benchmark Scenario	-	*31%*	*31%*	*26%*	*26%*	*29%*	*26%*	*23%*	*20%*	*11%*	*11%*	*3%*	*0%*
Return on Gross Revenue	*28%*	*24%*	*24%*	*27%*	*27%*	*25%*	*26%*	*28%*	*29%*	*28%*	*28%*	*33%*	*34%*
Total developer return after paying off all costs (incl. land cost) - PV	***$190***	***$70***	***$80***	***$80***	***$80***	***$90***	***$90***	***$90***	***$100***	***$140***	***$140***	***$160***	***$160***
% Reduction from Benchmark Scenario	-	*63%*	*58%*	*58%*	*58%*	*53%*	*53%*	*53%*	*47%*	*26%*	*26%*	*16%*	*16%*
Return on Gross Revenue	*15%*	*7%*	*8%*	*8%*	*8%*	*9%*	*9%*	*9%*	*11%*	*13%*	*13%*	*15%*	*15%*

*Note that in some instances where land value has been capitalized by an existing use, there may still be a book value to land that must be acknowledged. This will be variable from site to site.

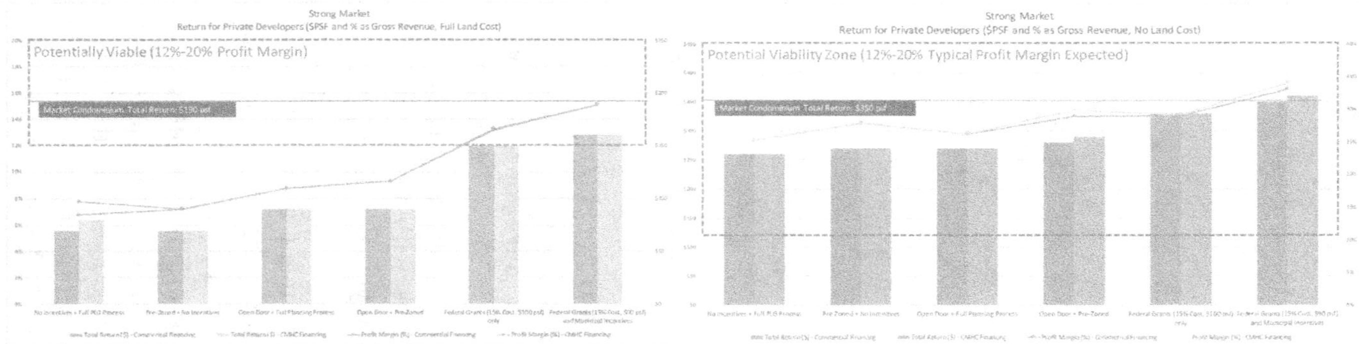

Figure 1.14 - Profitability

By stacking some of the available incentive programs, you can still make the returns you're expecting. If a joint venture is created with a landowner, some of the land costs go down, making it even more financially favourable.

Figure 1.15 - Development Analysis

Conclusion

There is a huge opportunity here. I would encourage developers to take a close look at all current programs. If you are an owner, leveraging the sites you own and making partnerships with the municipality also helps. It benefits everyone if you are viewed as part of the housing solution.

Many apartment owners have older buildings with excess space that can be utilized for more density. However, these people are now second- and third-generation owners—no longer the original builders. They would make good joint venture partners for developers (who can bring their development skills to the table). Owners have property management skills and land. Often, the land is enough equity to build the deal, with the right kind of capital stack in place.

What we find most interesting is, part of the capital stack could be seed funding and grant funding. However, a municipality may have reasons to oppose such a project because of Yellow Belt policies that under-zone these properties. However, by bringing affordability to the table, the municipality might be amenable to see these projects through because they align with their affordable housing push.

2

Where and What to Build

Introduction

In the not-too-distant past, affordable housing was not top of mind for most developers. However, the social, economic, and political climates have undergone profound changes. Today, the majority of clients who approach us are interested in affordable housing. They want to take advantage of government incentives and grants, but are uneducated about the many factors that come into play in order to succeed.

It's not just about applying for a grant. It's about the developer ensuring the design works for a grant, but also works for them in the long term by minimizing equity and having an adequate coverage ratio, whether they're planning to keep or sell.

Many developers are concerned about unit sizing and unit mix. How are these affected by affordable housing requirements? Will a typical rental building design still work for affordable housing, or are changes necessary?

Developers need to know how much rent can be charged, whether electricity, water, and heating/cooling sub-metering will work, how parking requirements are affected, what minimum amenities are needed, and what level of finish and features is expected. These decisions become more complex when combining affordable housing units with standard rental units in the same project.

Our feasibility studies focus on five questions:

1. Should you build?
2. What should you build?
3. *What's the depth of the market?*
4. How much rent can be charged?
5. *How much will the building be worth?*

Question 3 can be answered quickly: there is no limit to the depth of the market. Realistically, you can continue to build affordable housing and there will always be waiting lists. (However, not in all cases. Under the CMHC Residential Construction Financing initiative (RCFi), the average rent is 90% of the market rent, as determined by an appraisal report. This means that some of the unit rents would be above 90% and others below. Therefore, if the appraisal report is bullish, some of the units will be renting at or close to market, and there is a vacancy risk for units closer to 100% market rent.)

Question 5 will be covered in detail in Chapter 3, "Government Grants and Financing for Affordable Housing." It will cover financial goals and the difference between an affordable building versus a market rate building.

This leaves the remaining three questions for us to bring into sharper focus.

Question 1. Should you Build?

Yes! Affordable housing is a huge opportunity for developers. It makes sense for them to pivot from conventional rental, or any other asset class, into affordable housing. However, there are some considerations to keep in mind.

Considerations

CONSIDERATION	SOLUTION
Different Operating Model	There are professional property managers well versed in this
Working with government agencies	Grants and agreements require ongoing maintenence - ensure there's someone in your organization who has dedicated hours to this with experience
Duration of agreement - Inflation	Understand historic rate increases and use this
Limitation on rents	Look at historic rate increases and put into proforma

Figure 2.1 - Building Considerations

Affordable housing is truly a different operating model. Property managers must be well versed in affordable housing issues. Residents with varying health/social requirements typically require health services, and employment/social support services, close by. In the past, affordable housing buildings have contained social service offices on the ground floor, such as government or nonprofit, instead of commercial/retail space (though tenants of RCFi with rent an average 10% lower than market will behave closer to regular market tenants).

After working with government agencies from the building's inception to completion, developers will still send ongoing reports to different levels of government. This takes time and a certain amount of expertise. Typically, developers will need someone dedicated to this process. A property manager with this expertise will make a developer/owner's work far easier.

Both rents and expenses are typically tied to whichever program was used. Rather than just the typical 2% or 3% yearly inflation on rent, the pro forma must also consider historical municipal/provincial/federal rent guidelines.

Benefits

SHOULD I BUILD? THE BENEFITS

- Guaranteed lease-up
- Municipal concessions (we'll discuss these)
- Preferrable financing options (Chapter 3)
- Growing demand from buyers
- Limited turnover

Figure 2.2 - The Benefits

With affordable housing, the affordable portion's lease-up is mainly guaranteed. There will be a municipal waiting list to draw from—a building will be full from day one, as long as everything is in place to ensure this happens.

Municipal concessions do differ from municipality to municipality. They can include limited parking requirements, cash-in-lieu of parkland, development charges (DCs), and property tax rebates. It may also include a reduction or elimination of parkland dedication fees. All of these benefits add up within your pro forma.

Preferable financing options will be covered further in Chapter 3, "Government Grants and Financing for Affordable Housing."

With a growing demand from buyers, affordable housing is set to become a tradable asset in Canada. It is wise for developers to take advantage of this growing trend now.

In a typical market rental building, some turnover is desirable to ensure that rents can be raised on an annual basis. However, this results in a lot of wear and tear, and extra staffing costs associated with turnover. In an affordable building, renters will typically stay for the duration of their tenancy or duration of your agreement (which could be 10 years or more). This is a definite plus when staffing a stabilized building. On the negative side, if tenants in the affordable units stay for long periods, the developer will not be able to benefit from increases at turnover stages.

Where to Build

- Limited parking
- Proximity to transit
- More affordable land prices
  (pro forma rents will be more limited)
- Municipal priority areas

Figure 2.3 - Where to Build

For affordable housing, not every site is created equally. Developers should consider sites with limited parking, and if possible, surface parking. Where land prices are high, digging down more than one storey is not viable. With limited parking, sites must have a good transit score, and are usually only attractive to student housing. However, these sites may work quite well for affordable housing.

Proximity to transit often gives a developer an edge over other developers looking to get municipal grants for affordable housing. This is because the municipality knows that most tenants will not own a car, limiting parking needs. Proximity to transit will improve the attractiveness of a site for municipal grants—it also improves tenant satisfaction.

Developers should look for a site that is more affordable so the pro forma will support rents that are about 80% to 90% (in the case of RCFi financing) of market rent.

Some municipalities do have priority areas. You can find these within the community improvement plans (CIPS). This should be a developer's first port of call.

An Example Market

In Kitchener, a secondary market within southwestern Ontario, the incentives provided by the municipality for affordable housing only apply to building sites within the shaded areas below.

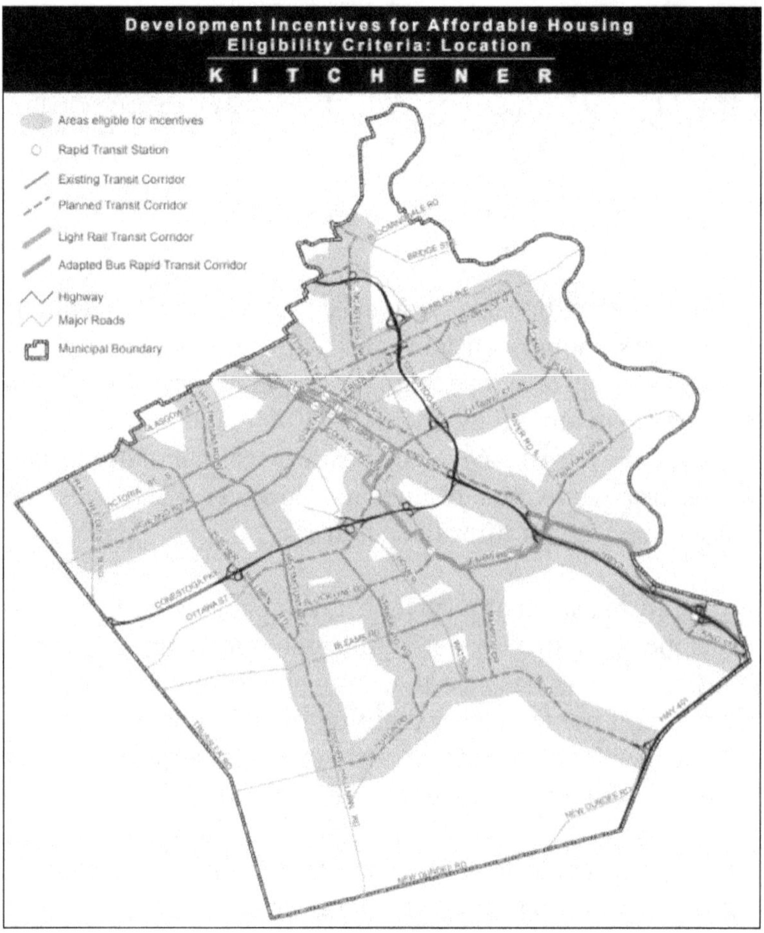

Figure 2.4 - Eligible Areas

A developer is more than welcome to develop affordable housing in any other part of Kitchener, but they will not be eligible for those municipal incentives, which are parkland dedication fees, waving development charges, and lesser parking requirements.

Question 2. What Should I Build ?

What to build can be quite a detailed discussion. However...

Your first port of call should always be the program guidelines.

All municipalities will have a developer's website or developer's package that will outline their goals, their expectations from developers, and any concessions they are willing to give. If you cannot find these, call or email the municipality.

The right relationship between rental rate, construction cost and permitted density is a key factor of what to build. For instance, low rental rates will only allow wood-frame construction buildings with densities of up to four storeys.

It would be a waste of time attempting to begin a project before knowing what the municipality expects for an affordable housing project. Here is a general guide for unit mix and sizing.

- Affordable rents are typically a "flat rate"per unit
- It is not necessarily in your best interest to exceed the minimum unit sizes
- Rent per square foot will decrease with large unit sizes
- Maximize one-bedroom units within the allowances of program guidelines

Figure 2.5 - Unit Mix & Sizing

Affordable rents are typically a flat rate per unit. (However, in the RFCi program, market rents are determined based on rent per square foot multiplied by the unit's square footage.) Municipalities will want a one-bedroom unit to be a certain rental rate and, a two-bedroom unit to be a different rate. Because of this, a developer will want to make those units as small as possible. This may sound a bit harsh, but a pro forma is run on a rent per square foot basis. If the rent is limited, then it makes sense to limit the square footage.

Some municipalities do require a set proportion of one-, two-, and three-bedroom units. However, most don't. Most are just looking for additional affordable housing.

It is important to maximize the number of one-bedroom units and minimize the square footage to improve the pro forma. If you want to do a 50-50 split between one-bedroom and two-bedroom units, the key is to compare rent per square foot to cost per square foot to confirm which unit type is cheaper.

An Example

This is from the city of Toronto, Ontario.

3.2 Unit Mix, Size and Location

3.2.1. 40% of all housing units should contain one bedroom and be no less than 525 sq ft (48.7 sq m) in area. The average of all one bedroom affordable units will be no less than 590 square feet (55 sq m) (+/-5%). Bachelor units are not acceptable.

3.2.2. 40% of all units should contain two bedrooms and should be no less than 650 sq ft (60 sq m) in area. The average size of all two bedroom units should be 725 square feet (+/-5%).

3.2.3. 15% of all units should contain three bedrooms and should be no less than 900 sq ft (84 sq m) in area. The average size of three bedroom units should be 1000 square feet (+/-5%).

3.2.4. 5% of all units should contain four bedrooms and should be no less than 1100 sq ft (102 sq m) in area. The average size of all four bedroom units shall be 1175 square feet (+/-5%).

3.2.5. Family Units:

a. Larger family units are preferred either on the ground floor with direct access to a street with front door space; or
b. In building types that don't permit this configuration, family units can also function well on a podium (above grade) with an outdoor terrace.
c. Family units should have proportionally larger living, dining and storage areas.
d. Outdoor private amenity spaces such as patios, balconies and terraces are key features for family suites.

3.2.6. Bedrooms should be a minimum of 100 sq ft (9.3 sq m) with a minimum dimension of 9 ft and include operable windows to the exterior.

Figure 2.6 - Example of Toronto Requirements

Toronto has very specific guidelines for the percentage of bachelor units, one-bedroom units, two-bedroom units, three-bedroom units, etc. They are also specific as to minimum unit sizes. If a developer is considering building affordable housing in Toronto, they must build units at those minimum square footages and adhere, very specifically, to the unit mix percentage guideline.

Most municipalities are not like Toronto. They don't normally have a very specific breakdown of unit mix and sizing.

Note: It's always worth asking what the current guidelines are and if they are willing to change them for a particular project. The last thing a developer needs is to complete architectural plans and spend money on a feasibility study and consulting for a building not designed to guidelines from the beginning.

Commercial Components

Most developments, particularly in more urban areas, do have some commercial space on the ground floor. However, there are limits to the financing available for affordable housing when commercial space is added.

- There are limits to CMHC financing with commercial components
- Some municipal programs don't allow commercial
- You must check the guidelines!

Figure 2.7 - What About Commercial

In the GTA (Greater Toronto Area), CMHC has limits for commercial space when part of an affordable plan. Some municipal programs do not allow any commercial space at all. Before considering commercial space, developers must find out the CMHC and municipality's limits.

Is All Affordable OK?

The percentage of affordable units does vary by program.

DO I HAVE TO BUILD ALL AFFORDABLE?

- Dependent on programs being applied for
- Most will have a minimum requirement
- There may be preferential treatment of applications with a higher proportion of affordable – ASK YOUR REP!

Figure 2.8 - Do I Have to Build All Affordable

Most do not require you to build 100% affordable. However, from an application standpoint, there can be preferential treatment for applications with a higher proportion of affordable.

CMHC is quite clear about this, but ask whether the minimum is really a minimum, or whether there is a preferred percentage for you to include.

A Case Study: Kitchener

For these affordable units, there is an exemption from development, application fees, and building permit fees. There are also deferred development charge payments, and preference for parking requirements. To qualify, you must have a minimum of 20% of residential units as affordable—80% below average market rent.

20% is a very low figure. There are programs across Canada that can go up to 50% (which need significant municipal concessions). These will need careful calibration within your pro forma.

The Keeping or Selling Implications

In any real estate transaction, a pure play deal is better than two asset classes mixed together.

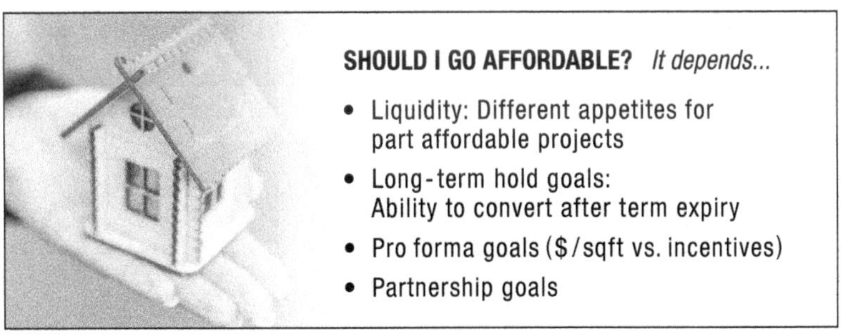

Figure 2.9 - Should I Go Affordable?

When selling an apartment building, or a building that is 50% retail and 50% apartments, who will be the buyer? Is this a retail deal or a rental deal? A 10% or 15% retail building does not cause a financing problem. The reverse is also true. A retail space with a few apartments on the top floor is still a very workable deal.

We believe that, as this market develops, there will be an opportunity to go 100% affordable—and this will be desired by the buyer who has an affordable fund. Right now, there are limits on the amount of money available from the municipality. Assuming we move forward, and this becomes a movement, we will see more pure luxury deals and more pure affordable deals.

Quirky Sites

A site may not need to be A-Class or B-Class land like a conventional luxury apartment. This site could be called "quirky."

Quirky sites are not ideal to get top-of-the-market rent; the target might be more middle-market rents.

Mixing Affordable and Market Rental

With 100% affordable, it is easy to make a building into stacks. Nevertheless, when mixing affordable with market, we must think very carefully about the full plans and which units are assigned to affordable versus market units.

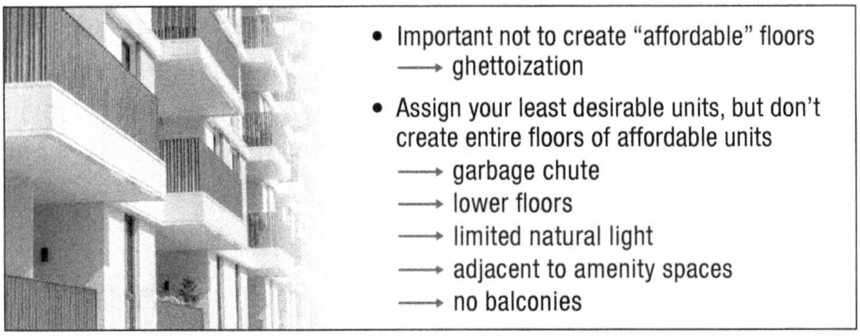

Figure 2.10 - Avoiding the Affordable Stack

It is important not to assign entire floors to affordable rent. At some point, word will get out, and potential/existing renters will feel that they are living in a split social housing/market rent building.

The typical advice is to disperse the affordable residents across unit types. Using the same strategy as when assigning each unit a market rental rate, the less desirable units can be assigned as affordable. Factors such as proximity to garbage chute, adjacent to noisy amenities, lower floor units, limited view or less natural light, and lack of balcony can be taken into consideration.

Fit and Finish

A unit built to the fit-and-finish standard of the image below is a bit of a cliche—but it is how many picture what affordable housing looks like.

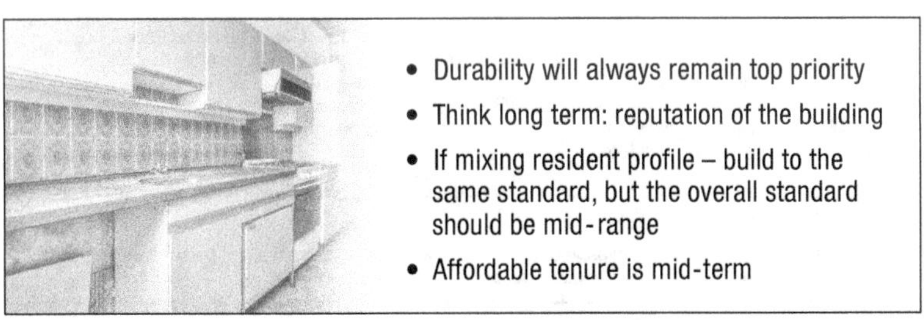

Figure 2.11 - What Not To Build

While a developer might want to keep costs to a minimum, they do not want their units to look or feel cheap. This will sully their reputation. The developer wants to rent a large percentage of market units at premium prices. A good reputation is vital to achieving this goal.

With a mixed resident profile, is it wise to outfit the affordable units differently than market units? No.

It is not in your best interest to do this for a couple of reasons. One, you might as well just buy 100% of everything rather than splitting your contracts 20-80. Two, if you think long term —affordable tenure is typically your mid-term option rather than your long-term option— and you have a 10- or 20-year agreement, the ability to sell after that time will depend on the condition of the units. Having them all at the same higher standard will support a high asking price.

Municipal Guidelines

Always check municipal guidelines. Not every municipality has guidelines available, but some of the larger ones do, as in Toronto's very specific guideline below.

3.3 Common Space

3.3.1. Building entrances/waiting/lobby areas should provide:

a. Comfortable areas for tenants to sit, socialize, and wait for vehicular pick-up.
b. Comfortable seating and space to accommodate persons with mobility devices.
c. Clear sightlines to the vehicular entrance and arrival area.
d. Areas around elevators should have additional space for people to wait either in seating provided or on mobility devices. Where space is tight, pull-down chairs might be considered.

3.3.2. Main entries should provide automatic door openers on both exterior entrance and related vestibule doors.

3.3.1. Amenity space and washrooms should be accessible to seniors and persons with varying disabilities. Provide automatic door openers in these rooms.

Figure 2.12 - More Toronto Guidelines

Amenities

A developer might say, "I'm putting in amenities to drive my rent, but I can't drive my rents because this is affordable housing and the rent I can charge is fixed. So why would I include amenities at all?" The answer is that amenities are extremely location specific.

Again, check municipal guidelines. The City of Toronto has minimum guidelines as to what must be included—typically a lobby and some social space.

Think Longer Term

- In a mixed resident profile building, you must cater to your market rent residents
- In a strictly affordable resident profile building, you'll need some resident service space that can be converted, after-the-fact, into market rent amenity space
- CARVE OUT THE AMENITY SPACE NOW!

Figure 2.13 - Carve Out Amenity Space in the Beginning

If you have both market rental and affordable residents, create a building that is going to cater to the market residents rather than the affordable residents. The pro forma should also reflect market rather than affordable.

If a building will be 100% affordable, how can some specific spaces be carved out for amenity space down the road. Maybe a one-bedroom unit could be redeployed as a co-working space, a lounge, or a social space. When converted, the building becomes viable for market rental.

Parking

Parking is a sticky issue. Many municipalities will provide incredibly low parking requirements for affordable housing. This works well for "quirky" sites. If there are strict limitations on underground parking, affordable could be the best way to proceed.

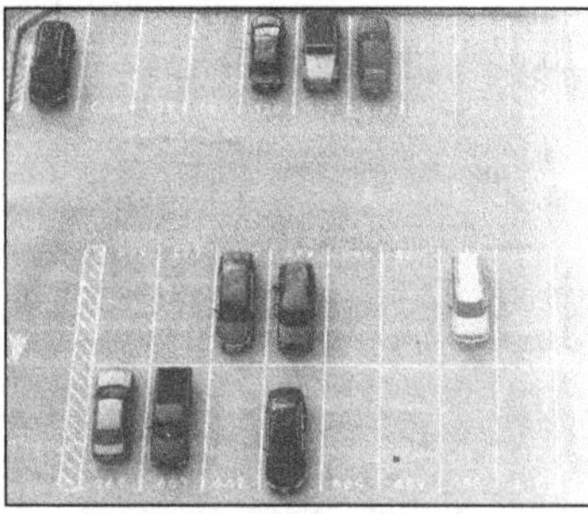

- Many municipalities offer parking concessions for affordable housing
- Be careful if you want to switch to market rent upon expiry
- Talk to your broker about a buyer who wants to take on the building long term as affordable if you're doing limited parking

Figure 2.14 - Plan Parking Carefully

In the long term, the lack of parking will become an issue. If the plan is to reposition from affordable to market rental, the limited parking will affect the ability to attract the highest rents.

Parking Case Study: Kamloops, BC

KAMLOOPS AFFORDABLE HOUSING
DEVELOPERS' PACKAGE
Page 9

Reduced Parking Requirements

The City's parking requirements were updated in 2010 to reflect parking demand trends. Parking requirements for multi-family housing are now based on bedroom count, while requirements for social housing and seniors housing are less than those for other residential uses. (e.g. for social housing the parking requirement is 0.25 spots per unit).

To be eligible:

- A development needs to be one of the types designated in the bylaw (multiple-family social housing, multiple-family dwellings, seniors housing, or bachelor suites). Affordable and seniors housing developments require a housing agreement.

To apply:

- Parking requirements are reviewed at the Development Permit and/or Building Permit stage. As is the case for tax and DCC exemptions, it is best to contact the Development and Engineering Services Department early in your project to discuss these opportunities.

For current parking requirements, please see Division Fifty-Two of Kamloops Zoning Bylaw No. 5-1-2001, available at:
https://kamloops.civicweb.net/Documents/DocumentList.aspx?ID=10621

Figure 2.15 - Kamloops Requirements

Like many other municipalities, Kamloops will negotiate the parking structure. A developer should check all municipal requirements carefully before going to their architect.

Question 4.
How Much Can I Charge in Rent?

As the primary source of income and highly influencing the value of the building, the rent charged must be as high as possible. In the affordable housing market, most developers are layering multiple incentive programs.

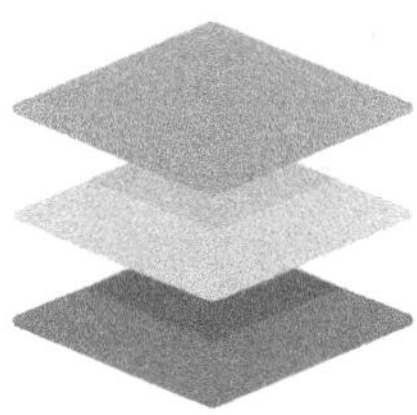

HOW MUCH CAN I CHARGE IN RENT?

- It's fixed – and increases are based on annual guidelines from the program
- If layering programs, you must provide the lowest rent

Figure 2.16 - Layered Incentives

Typically, developers take advantage of CMHC programs along with municipal and provincial initiatives. Unless there is something specifically within the guidelines stating that those programs work hand in hand, they always need to price units based on the lowest rents. If CMHC provides a certain level of rent, and BC housing (for example) provides some level of rent, but the municipality requires the lowest rent of all those, in order to qualify for these three programs, the developer must go with the lowest rent level.

As a developer, it is important to think very carefully about whether it is worth taking on one or more programs. This requires playing around with the pro forma to understand the benefits that come from that lowest rent and whether it actually makes sense.

UNIT SIZE	2021 AVG MARKET RENT	2021 80% OF AVG MARKET RENT
Hostel	$942	$754
Bachelor apartment	$1,211	$969
1-bedroom apartment	$1,431	$1,145
2-bedroom apartment	$1,661	$1,329
3-bedroom apartment	$1,896	$1,517
4-bedroom apartment	$2,194	$1,755
5-bedroom apartment	$2,454	$1,963
2-bedroom townhouse	$1,988	$1,590
3-bedroom townhouse	$1,928	$1,542
4-bedroom townhouse	$2,546	$2,037
5-bedroom townhouse	$2,945	$2,356

Figure 2.17 - Toronto AMR

This rent guideline is from the city of Toronto. It gives an idea about the average market rent and 80% of that rent. This is typically what an agreement would allow. As you can see, pertinent to unit mix and sizing, it doesn't matter if a one-bedroom apartments is 500, 525, or 600 square feet, a set amount of rent must be charged.

Utilities

We're often asked whether or not to sub-meter utilities. Normally, we recommend sub-metering for all new rental developments.

UNIT SIZE	HYDRO	HEAT	WATER	HOT WATER
Bachelor apartment	$34	$26	$11	$19
1-bedroom apartment	$34	$26	$11	$19
2-bedroom apartment	$49	$30	$21	$26
3-bedroom apartment	$57	$31	$25	$32
4-bedroom apartment	$61	$31	$28	$40
5-bedroom apartment	$61	$31	$28	$40
2-bedroom townhouse	$49	$30	$21	$26
3-bedroom townhouse	$57	$31	$25	$32
4-bedroom townhouse	$61	$31	$28	$40
5-bedroom townhouse	$61	$31	$28	$40

Figure 2.18 - Utility Allowances

Realistically, in many municipalities, as a developer or property owner for affordable housing, you can charge for that sub-metering, but it comes off your rent.

In the longer term, especially if repositioning to market rents, sub-metering is the way to go. If you intend to sell the building, perhaps it's not in your best interest. It's something to discuss very carefully with your broker and with the sub-metering company.

Case Study: Worksheet

This is a very useful worksheet that looks at all of the different factors mentioned.

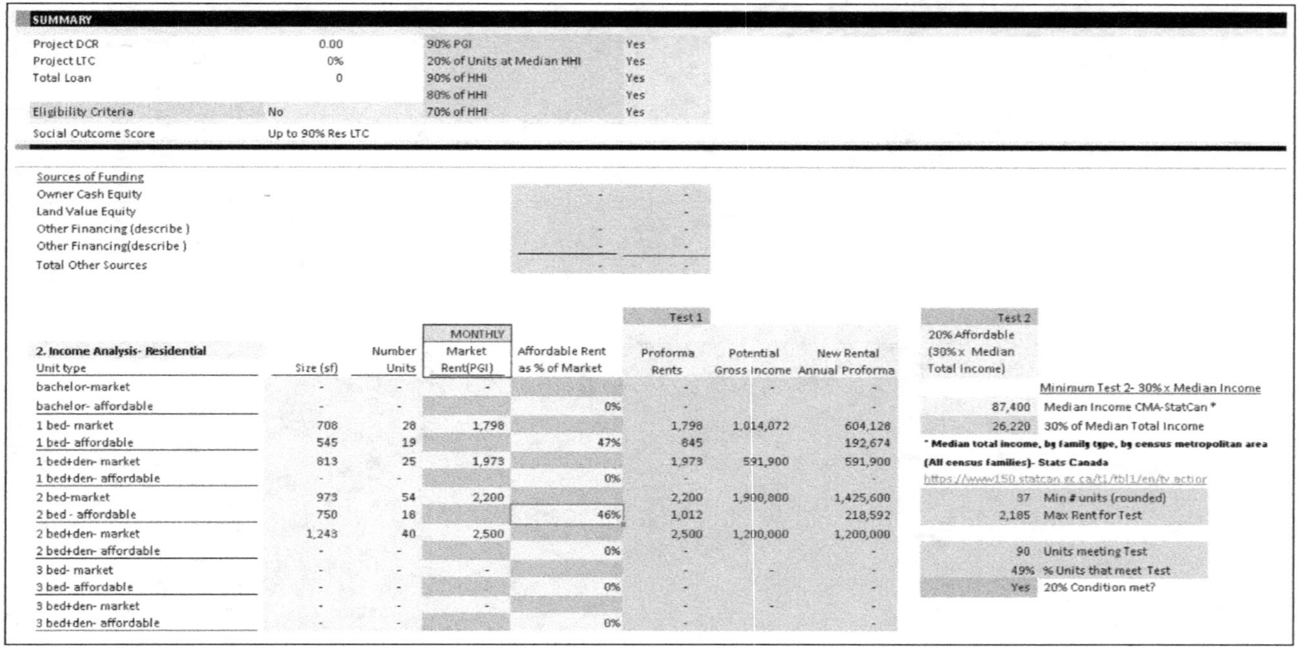

SUMMARY			
Project DCR	0.00	90% PGI	Yes
Project LTC	0%	20% of Units at Median HHI	Yes
Total Loan	0	90% of HHI	Yes
		80% of HHI	Yes
Eligibility Criteria	No	70% of HHI	Yes
Social Outcome Score	Up to 90% Res LTC		

Sources of Funding			
Owner Cash Equity	-	-	-
Land Value Equity			-
Other Financing (describe)		-	-
Other Financing(describe)		-	-
Total Other Sources		-	-

2. Income Analysis- Residential Unit type	Size (sf)	Number Units	MONTHLY Market Rent(PGI)	Affordable Rent as % of Market	Test 1 Proforma Rents	Potential Gross Income	New Rental Annual Proforma
bachelor-market	-	-	-		-	-	-
bachelor- affordable	-	-		0%	-		-
1 bed- market	708	28	1,798		1,798	1,014,072	604,128
1 bed- affordable	545	19		47%	845		192,674
1 bed+den- market	813	25	1,973		1,973	591,900	591,900
1 bed+den- affordable	-	-		0%	-		-
2 bed-market	973	54	2,200		2,200	1,900,800	1,425,600
2 bed - affordable	750	18		46%	1,012		218,592
2 bed+den- market	1,243	40	2,500		2,500	1,200,000	1,200,000
2 bed+den- affordable	-	-		0%	-		-
3 bed- market	-	-	-		-	-	-
3 bed- affordable	-	-		0%	-		-
3 bed+den- market	-	-	-		-	-	-
3 bed+den- affordable	-	-		0%	-		-

Test 2 20% Affordable (30% x Median Total Income)	Minimum Test 2- 30% x Median Income
87,400	Median Income CMA-StatCan *
26,220	30% of Median Total Income
37	Min # units (rounded)
2,185	Max Rent for Test
90	Units meeting Test
49%	% Units that meet Test
Yes	20% Condition met?

*** Median total income, by family type, by census metropolitan area (All census families)- Stats Canada**

https://www150.statcan.gc.ca/t1/tbl1/en/tv.actior

Figure 2.19 - CMHC Worksheet

When considering unit mix and sizing, market rents, amenity space, commercial space, etc., it will show whether a project meets the minimum requirements in terms of income, unit mix and sizing, rents, etc. It will also result in a score that informs us if a development will have priority within the waiting list for affordable housing.

We'd be happy to go into details with anyone interested.

Conclusion

It makes sense for developers to pivot from conventional rental, or any other asset class, into affordable housing, as the opportunity awaiting them is huge. With the right mix of affordability, unit sizes, amenities, parking, and utilities, it is financially viable for the longer term.

Municipalities do have information available to help developers plan—laying out expectations and any concessions they are willing to give. Additionally, developers can access multiple incentive programs from other levels of government; mixing and matching to help them meet their own goals.

3

Government Grants and Financing for Affordable Housing

Government grants and the financing of affordable housing are critical parts of this business. Unfortunately, the current programs are not going to solve the affordable housing crisis. The federal government has only allocated $1 billion. That only builds about 3,000 apartments. If leveraged, it might build about a 10th of those apartments.

There must be more initiatives—and we believe more are coming. Our position is that developers, and the industry as a whole, must prepare for, what we think, is a significant opportunity. Most developers will be surprised how profitable building affordable housing is.

Our current housing crisis took about 40 years to create. It's going to take some time to remedy. Good policies plus private capital plus developer involvement are what is needed. Government alone cannot solve this problem.

Affordable Housing Programs in Toronto

Toronto's Open Door Affordable Housing Program from 2010 to 2019 set out to build 10,000 new homes over 10 years, but only completed 4,093—about 40% of the target.

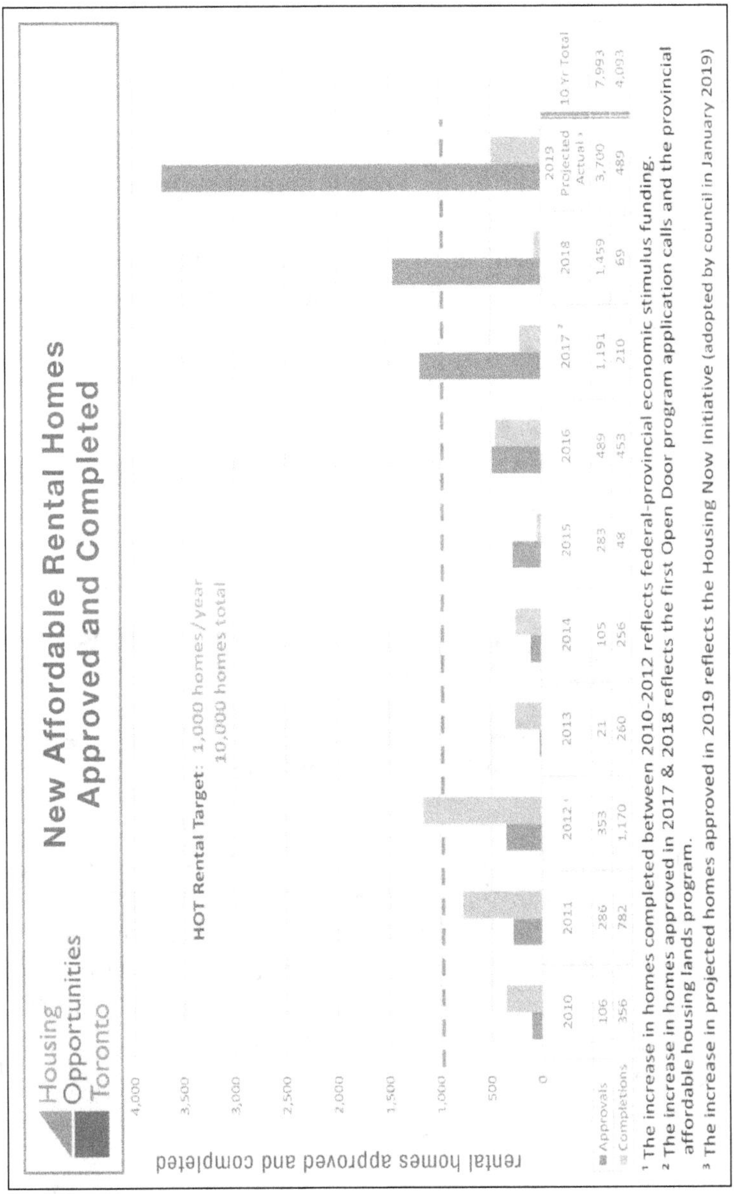

Figure 3.1 - Affordable Rentals in Toronto

However, in 2019, there were 3,700 approvals—a huge increase over the preceding years. This indicates an increased momentum for affordable housing. We see this momentum continuing.

Maturing Agreements

There are 8,500 units under former federal housing providers in properties that are nearing the expiry of their operating agreements, and another 18,000 affordable units administered under provincial legislation whose mortgages will expire beginning in 2022 and continuing to 2032.

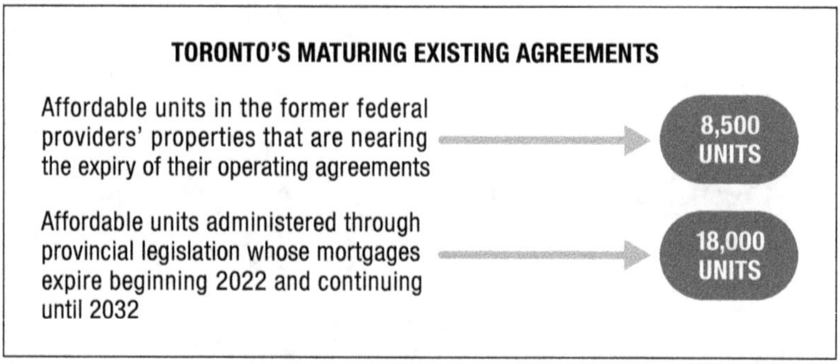

Figure 3.2 - Maturing Agreements

After housing providers' operating agreements and mortgages mature, the relationship between the provider and the city ends. Therefore, there is a risk that the housing units will not remain affordable. Preserving the affordable housing stock after those agreements end is a key issue facing the city. The dire need for new affordable rental units is reflected in the city's 2020 to 2030 new affordable rental targets.

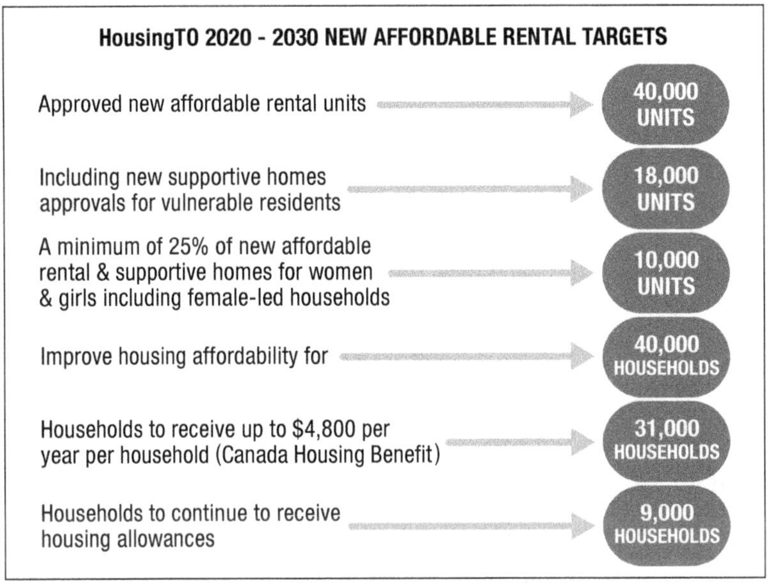

Figure 3.3 - Affordable Rental Targets

The city plans to approve 40,000 new affordable rental units in this period. This is a comprehensive, well-studied program. The 40,000 units include new 18,000 supportive homes for vulnerable residents. Also, the program provides that, of the 40,000 units, at least 25% will be allocated to women and girls, including female-led households.

Additional targets include improving the housing affordability for 40,000 households.

Of these, 31,000 households will receive a Canada Housing Benefit up to $4,800 per year per household to assist with rental costs. This benefit will be paid directly to the household and is fully portable. Also, 9,000 households will continue to receive housing allowances.

The Toronto Open Door program complements other federal, provincial, and city housing funding programs, and provides for exemptions from planning fees, development charities, fast-tracking planning approvals, activating surplus and public lands for portable housing.

KEY FEATURES OF THE TORONTO OPEN DOOR PROGRAM

As a part of the City of Toronto's *Housing Now Initiative*, 17 sites have been identified to create affordable rental housing as part of mixed-income and complete communities. More information is available at **www.toronto.ca/affordablehousing**

Figure 3.4 - Open Door Key Features

As part of the city's housing initiative, 17 sites have been identified to create affordable rental housing as part of mixed-income and complete communities. For more information, please visit the city's website as this information is continually updated.

- Process ran from OCT 2020 to JAN 2021
- Staff recommended 971 new affordable homes in 15 developments
- 11 of the 15 developments are proposed by nonprofit housing providers (3 of these 11 are indigenous)
- Many cases of the recommendations will be affordable in perpetuity (program requires minimum 40 years affordability)

NOTE: PLEASE VISIT THE CITY OF TORONTO'S WEBSITE FOR MORE INFO: www.toronto.ca/news/971-new-affordable-homes-to-be-created-through-the-city-of-torontos-2020-call-for-open-door-affordable-housing-program-applications

Figure 3.5 - Open Door Call Results

The city issues, and then will call for, affordable rental housing applications to ensure a competitive process. Applicants are required to submit a complete Open Door application package within certain timelines as per the call.

The city has established an interdivisional Open Door review committee to streamline the Open Door program approvals. The results show that 11 of the 15 developments are proposed by nonprofit housing providers, which means that they could only approve a maximum of four applications from the for-profit sector.

Overall, only 971 new affordable rental homes were approved. This shows the immense opportunity remaining in this sector for the for-profit industry. Please visit the city's website for more information.

Other Requirements

In our model, we're assuming 100% affordable housing.

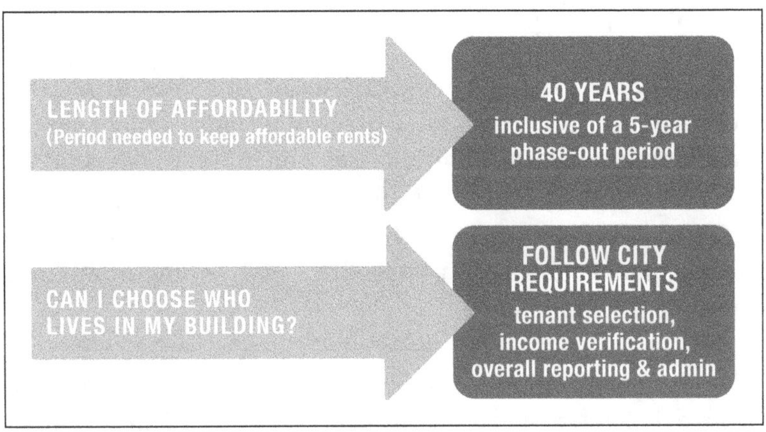

Figure 3.6 - Other Requirements

Affordable rental is secured for a minimum of 40 years. Market rents can be charged during the last five years of a phase-out period upon vacancy subject to provincial legislation. To ensure compliance, the city requires a detailed contribution agreement to be signed and a charge created on the asset. You must follow the city's requirements as to the selection of tenants.

City incentives include exemption from: fees and charges, planning application fees, development charges, building permit fees, education development charges for the Toronto District School Board (TDSB), parkland dedication fees, and residential property taxes during the affordability period.

1. Exemption from fees and charges
2. Planning application fees & development charges
3. Building permit fees, education development charges (TDSB)
4. Parkland dedication fees
5. Residential property taxes (duration of affordability)
6. Capital funding
7. Planning help: open door planning service

Figure 3.7 - Incentives

The city does not provide exemption for fees from (but not limited to): Toronto District Catholic School Board development charges, public art contribution, Section 37 contributions, hydro levies, fees related to urban forestry, technical service fees, right of permit fees including landscape, construction permits, city occupation, and municipal road damage.

The city has funding available for affordable rental housing from a dedicated development charges reserve fund and must be justified by the developer. Generally, applicants requiring no funding or little funding will be more competitive, score higher in the process, and are more likely to be approved.

Projects approved through the Open Door program will be assigned a dedicated city-planning staff member to coordinate and facilitate the development review process within city planning, the Aboriginal Housing Office (AHO), and other city divisions commenting on the development application.

The application is to include:

- Details of the proposed project
- Development qualifications
- Management qualifications
- Corporate financial viability
- Project design and a confirmation of the required pre-application meeting with city planning
- Development schedule
- Capital and operating financial plans
- Community consultation and communications outreach plan

Again, please refer to the city's website for up-to-date details in the decision-making process, including its negotiation processes, as they can change at any time.

Overview of Financing Programs

CMHC is driven by social outcomes: affordability, financial viability, energy efficiency, and accessibility.

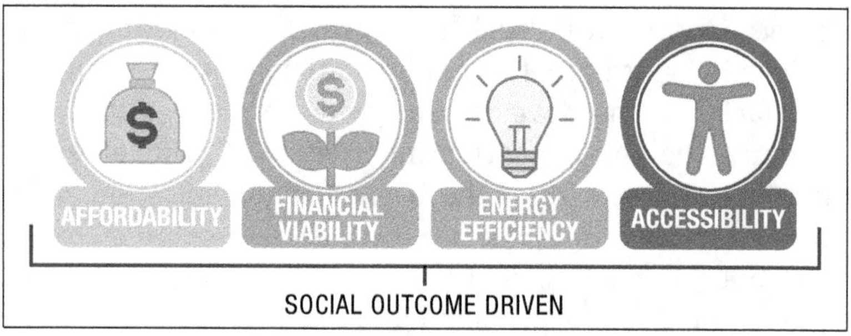

Figure 3.8 - Minimum Mandatory Requirements

We'll only focus on affordability.

Figure 3.9 - Affordability Definition

Affordability Definition 1

If a developer owns a site that they believe is fit for affordable housing, the first step is to conduct a pro forma of market rents. The reason for this is, once an understanding of market rents is reached, they can calculate the affordable definition: the total rental income must be 10% below the potential rental income.

Next, assume 20% of units will rent at or below 30% of the median household income for the region (available from StatCan). That calculation, alongside the feasibility study, enables the developer to conduct the debt service coverage and see if the numbers work, and is applicable for the application CMHC requires.

The government wants to ensure that the developer has a 10-year term in place. (The 10-year term matches the fixed rates and therefore the debt service coverage is able to sustain the debt.)

Affordability Definition 2

The second definition is from government proposals already approved, and other initiatives aimed at developing rental housing, such as grants, concessions, and an expedited planning processing. As before, a developer will have to maintain a 10-year term.

Note that, just because you have the best site for affordable housing, doesn't mean you are going to get approved through CMHC. CMHC has certain criteria.

- At least 5 years experience operating a similar property
- Excellent credit and repayment history
- Proof of a similar project completed on time and on budget (or a contractor with this record)
- A net worth of at least 25% of the value of the loan
- The ability to guarantee 100% of the loan during construction and lease-up

Figure 3.10 - CMHC Borrower Eligibility Criteria

They require at least five-years experience of operating a similar property. They also want to ensure that you have historical development experience and have built one or two properties on time and on budget.

If a developer does not have that experience, they may need to engage a consultant who does in order to have the best chance at getting approved. A developer must also have an excellent credit and repayment history, and have a net worth of at least 25% of the value of the loan to guarantee it.

Lastly, a developer will have to guarantee 100% of the loan during construction and lease-up.

During Construction

When applying to build affordable housing, it's prudent to run two scenarios:

1. Retain **Rock Advisors** on the feasibility side to run the affordable housing NOI as well as market. The reason is to put a contingency in place in case the numbers aren't viable for affordable housing, or in case the application is denied.
2. Look at what else is possible.

Let's compare market rents, and the debt structures or debt available today for market rents, in connection with our comparison to CMHC.

Term Loan	CMHC Standard (Market Rental)	CMHC Standard (Affordable Rental)	CMHC Direct Application Rental Construction & Financing / National Housing Co-Investment Fund: Affordability / Energy Efficiency / Accessibility Criteria	Bank / Institution	MIC
Loan to Cost	Up to 75%	Up to 95% Up to 75% (non-residential)	Up to 90-100% of Cost Up to 75% (non-residential)	Up to 80%	Up to 85%
Interest Rates	~COF + 175-225 (2.19-2.69%)	~COF + 175-225 (2.19-2.69%)	0.85% locked in for 10 years from the date of first advance	~Prime + 1.0 - 1.5% (3.45% - 3.95%)	5.5%
Term	Up to 2 years	Up to 2 years	10 years	Up to 2 years	Up to 2 years
Fees	Application Fees - $200 for the first 100 units, $100/unit thereafter (Max $55,000); Premium - up to 5.25%, Lender processing fees for CMHC (Standard): 0.25 - 0.50%	Application Fees - $200 for the first 100 units, $100/unit thereafter (Max $55,000); Premium - up to 3%, Lender processing fees for CMHC (Affordable Flex): 0.5-0.75%	After rent up, when the project has achieved the rental income used in the underwriting of the loan, the loan may become non-recourse to the borrowers and guarantors	0.25 - 75%	1.00%
Guarantee	100%	100%	100%	100%	100%

Figure 3.11 - Comparing Borrowing

Loan to Cost

For market rental (market rents), CMHC will allow up to 75% total cost. The total costs definition is land, hard costs and soft costs, as well as reserves.

For CMHC affordable rental, you can go up to 95% loan to cost. However, if you have a nonresidential component (some cities require a retail component), you can go up to 75% loan to cost for the nonresidential component.

The CMHC Direct Application, also known as a National Housing Investment Fund that combines affordability, energy efficiency, and accessibility, allows you to go up to 100% loan to cost. The nonresidential component is capped at 75%.

Banks and institutions in this market will go as high as 80% (in a great location), but the norm is 75%.

Mortgage investment groups provide very competitive flex market rentals at 85% loan to cost using institutional capital. This lets the senior lender, like banks, trust companies with a mezzanine lender, and developer to combine them together. With that, we achieve 85% loan to cost—this is a very quick process.

Interest Rates

CMHC, whether it be market rental or affordable, is in the range of 1.62% to 2.69%. What's interesting about the CMHC Direct Application is they are able to lock in 0.85% for 10 years from the first advance—this is a very attractive option.

Banks and institutions range from prime +1 to prime +1.5, but this is comparing speed and flexibility versus time and economics.

Mortgage Investment Corporations (MICs) give more leverage at 5.5%—very economical.

Term

For CMHC market, the term is flexible across the board; it takes a couple of years to build most projects—get a two-year term. If the project is larger, it's possible to add another year for stabilization.

With CMHC affordable standard, you get up to two years.

For CMHC Direct Application, you automatically go to a 10-year term locking it in through a 10-year rate.

The banks, institutions, and the MICs are very similar in they offer a two year term. Again, if longer is needed for stabilization (to max out rents, max out the NOI, and make more profit), they will be amicable.

Fees

The fees for CMHC Market, Affordable, and Direct, are $200 for the first 100 units, $100 per unit thereafter.

Banks and institutions range from 0.25% to 0.75%, depending on the complexity and the market.

The MICs are typically at 1%. Remember, MICs are not giving up equity. So historically, a bank would give you, say, 75%. For developers who want to build two or three different projects at the same time, they must raise equity. Instead of diluting their equity position—which is the most expensive way—they can raise the debt and sustain the slightly higher fee.

Guarantees

Guarantees for construction are 100% across the board.

A Note on Cap Rates

Essentially, there are two interpretations of the cap rate. Meaning, it changes depending who's looking at it—lender versus buyer.

We think the buyer is going to be looking at sub threes. With brand new affordable housing, apartment building, and tenured terms, you're looking at sub fours.

Lenders will add a little more, between 10 to 30 basis points. However, this depends on the geographic region. We think it is safe to say the lenders will apply a slight premium to what the market's willing to buy.

We believe we have a general idea what those cap rates will be, but there's not enough significant data because so few affordable housing buildings trade. Apartment cap rates are low because of the stability and surety of income. Affordable rentals take that stability and surety to an even safer level. For that reason, you can expect affordable apartments to trade at less than a brand new market rent building right across the street.

Some developers may be hearing of cap rates between 2.5% and 3%. In downtown Toronto and Ottawa, that's a 40- to 50-year-old building. They may think their building is superior and should get a 2% cap rate. That is not the case. The reason the downtown cap rates are low is because there's an upside in the rents on turnover or excess land to build on. Those things are taken into consideration in the price—they are not paying that price because it is a better or worse building than yours.

The cap rate is not determined by the broker—it's determined by the market, likely because of stability. That's the inherent reason why developers are attracted to developing apartments. Affordable housing is even more stable than that. Thus, cap rate should be lower. But we need this product built—we need buyers and sellers to transact in this space.

Exit Strategy

The following table summarizes the exit strategies after construction is completed.

Term Loan	CMHC Standard (Market Rental)	CMHC Standard (Affordable Rental)	CMHC Direct Application Rental Construction & Financing / National Housing Co-Investment Fund: Affordability / Energy Efficiency / Accessibility Criteria	Bank / Institution
Loan to Value	Lesser of 85% or 100% of Cost	Lesser of 85% LTV or 100% of Cost	Up to 100% of Cost	Up to 75%
Interest Rates	~CMB + 100 = 1.79% 5yr ; 2.07% 10yr (Canadian Mortgage Bond) = 0.79/5 year & 1.07/10 year	~CMB + 100 = 1.79% 5yr; 2.07% 10yr (Canadian Mortgage Bond) = 0.79/5 year & 1.07/10 year	0.85% locked in for 10 years from the date of first advance	~5yr BA SWAP + 1% = 2.75% 5yr Note: 5yr BA = 1%
Term	Up to 10 years	Up to 10 years	Up to 10 years	Up to 10 years
Fees	Application Fees - $150 for the first 100 units, $100/unit thereafter (Max $55,000); Premium - up to 4.5-5.25% Lender processing fees for CMHC (Standard): 0.1-0.15% - No fees if rolling construction loan	Application Fees - $200 for the first 100 units, $100/unit thereafter (Max $55,000); Premium - up to 2.5%, Lender processing fees for CMHC (Affordable Flex): 0.1-0.15% - No fees if rolling construction loan	Application Fees - $200 for the first 100 units, $100/unit thereafter (Max $55,000)	0.10-0.15%
Guarantee	After 12 consecutive months of stabilized rent, the guarantee can be reduced 40% of the outstanding loan amount owing under the mortgage from time to time	After rent up, when the project has achieved the rental income used in the underwriting of the loan, the loan may become non-recourse to the borrowers and guarantors	After rent up, when the project has achieved the rental income used in the underwriting of the loan, the loan may become non-recourse to the borrowers and guarantors	Limited
Amortization	40 years	40 years	50 years	30 years
DSCR	1.20 (10 year), 1.30 (5 year)	1.10	1.10	1.15-1.25

Figure 3.12 - Exit Strategies

A Live Example

Assuming the same project is built both as affordable housing and market housing, this is how they pan out financially.

Market Rental

CONSTRUCTION FINANCING (BANK)			
Construction Loan	33,689,682	75%	2.50% Int Rate
Equity	11,000,000	25%	
Total	44,689,682	100%	
PERMANENT MORTGAGE FINANCING (CHMC)			
Restrictive Projected NOI on completion	2,159,975		
Loan capped at Loan to Cost Ratio of	100%	*OR*	
Loan to Value Ratio of	85%	*of market value*	
Annual Debt Service (including Principal)	1,768,522		
Max Allowed Principal Loan Value	44,689,682	*100% of Cost*	2.50% Int Rate
Market Value	53,999,378	*minimum required*	3.85% Cap Rate
CMHC DSCR (Restrictive projection)	1.20		
Actual DSCR	1.22		
Amortization (Years)	40		

Figure 3.13 - Market Rental

Affordable Housing

CONSTRUCTION FINANCING (CHMC)			
Construction Loan	33,004,043	95%	2.50% Int Rate
Equity	1,900,000	5%	
Total	34,904,043	100%	
PERMANENT MORTGAGE FINANCING (CHMC)			
Restrictive Projected NOI on completion	1,504,408		
Loan capped at Loan Value Ratio of	85%	*of market value*	
Annual Debt Service (including Principal)	1,314,399		
Max Allowed Principal Loan Value	33,214,212	*85% of MV*	2.50% Int Rate
Market Value	39,075,543	*39,075,543*	3.85% Cap Rate
CMHC DSCR (Restrictive projection)	1.10	*minimum required*	
Actual DSCR	1.14		
Amortization (Years)	40		

Figure 3.14 - Affordable Rental

The important differences are circled in orange.

Development Performance

These are the differences in the development performance of a hypothetical apartment built both as an affordable housing building and as a conventional rental.

Affordable Housing Building

For this comparison, we will be using the city of Toronto's Open Door program coupled with CMHC financing to illustrate a simple financial case study of an affordable apartment development that ticks all the boxes for federal, provincial, and municipal governments.

DEVELOPMENT SCENERIO - AFFORDABLE	
Building Size	125 units I 64k Net Rentable Square Feet
Market	Average Location
Land	Contributed at $100 PSF of NLA
Built Form	Precast
Incentives	CMHC Financing & City of Toronto

Figure 3.15 - Development Scenario

The building is 125 units precast of about 64,000 net rentable area, in an average location. Land is assumed to be contributed at $100 per square foot of usable area.

UNIT TYPE	AVG MONTHLY RENT (AMR)	UTILITY ALLOWANCE	AMR NET OF UTILITY ALLOWANCE
Bachelor apartment	$1,211	$90	$1,121
1-bedroom apartment	$1,431	$90	$1,341
2-bedroom apartment	$1,661	$126	$1,535
3-bedroom apartment	$1,896	$145	$1,751

Figure 3.16 - Toronto AMR for Affordable Housing

These are the 2021 Toronto average market rents (AMR) and the affordable housing utility allowances, which includes hydro, hot water, water, and heat in new development where utilities are sub-metered separately for each unit—residents pay the utility cost directly.

The maximum monthly rents are set at average monthly rent less an allowance for each separately metered utility (determined and updated annually by the city of Toronto). We will assume the AMR net of utility allowances for our development model.

UNIT TYPE	SQFT	# OF UNITS	% TOTAL	MONTHLY $	ANNUAL $	$/SQFT
Studio	410	40	32%	1,121	13,452	2.73
1-bedroom	535	70	56%	1,341	16,092	2.51
2-bedroom	700	15	12%	1,535	18,420	2.19
TOTAL	64,350	125	100%	161,735	1,940,820	2.51
AVERAGE	515	Res Only		1,294	15,527	2.51

OTHER INCOME			MONTHLY $	ANNUAL $
Laundry		$25	3,125	37,500
Parking Revenue	25 STALLS	x $100	2,500	30,000
TOTAL OTHER INCOME			5,625	67,500

		MONTHLY $	ANNUAL $
Total Potential Gross Revenue		167,360	2,008,320
Less: Vacancy and Collection Loss @	0.0%	–	–
EFFECTIVE GROSS INCOME		167,360	2,008,320

Figure 3.17 - Development Mix and Revenue

Assumptions

The apartment sizes are typical for Toronto. These are smaller sized units with low per square foot rates—$1,121 for the studio, $1,341 for one-bedroom and $1,535 for a two-bedroom. The blended average rate is $2.51 per square foot with an average rent of $1,294 per month.

We've assumed only 25 parking stalls (because this is an affordable development), which helps development cost. Note the 0% vacancy rate. The building will be occupied as soon as completed.

Operating Expenses

OPERATING EXPENSES	PER UNIT	%	PER SQFT	MONTHLY	ANNUAL $
Property Taxes	-	0%	-	-	-
Insurance	250	8%	0.49	2,604	31,250
Repair & Maintenance	750	23%	1.46	7,813	93,750
Utilitiest	900	28%	1.75	9,375	112,500
Staff (Ops & Maint)	650	20%	1.26	6,771	81,250
Gen Admin & Marketing	100	3%	0.19	1,042	12,500
Management Fee 3.5%	562	18%	1.09	5,858	70,291
TOTAL EXPENSES	3,212	100%	6.24	33,462	401,541

Figure 3.18 - Affordable Housing Expenses

Everything is standard, tailored for the affordable segment of the market. There is one exception: property taxes—they have been waived as an incentive.

Summary

DEVELOPMENT COSTS	TOTAL	PER UNIT	PER SQFT	%
Land	6,435,000	51,480	100	18.3%
Construction	22,972,950	286,744	357	65.3%
Professional Fees	1,193,400	9,547	19	3.4%
Development Management	496,003	3,968	8	1.4%
Permits and Approvals	257,400	2,059	4	0.7%
Marketing and Leasing	376,392	3,011	6	1.0%
Financing and Interest	1,606,952	27,657	25	4.6%
HST (Self Supply)	1,850,133	14,801	29	5.3%
TOTAL DEVELOPMENT COSTS	35,188,230	399,267	548	100%

Figure 3.19 - Affordable Development Costs Summary

The incentives, combined with simple construction, minimal parking, and reduced amenities, results in an overall construction cost of $542 per square foot net rentable area. (COVID-19 constraints to construction hard costs are not factored in.)

Return on Investment

NOI at stabilization	1,705,127
Capitalization Rate	3.85%
Valuation @ $2.67 per sqft avg rent	44,289,00
Less: Selling costs	(664,335)
Sales Proceeds	43,624,665
Total Cost	34,904,043
Profit before taxes if sold at stabilization	8,720,622
Return on cost	25.0%
Development Yield	4.9%
IRR upon stabilization if sold	87.0%
IRR 10-Year	35.4%
Construction Costs per unit	279,232
Construction costs per sqft	542
Value per unit at stabilization	354,312
Value per sqft at stabilization	688

Figure 3.20 - Affordable Return on Investment

We have used a 3.85% cap rate, which is slightly lower than a regular apartment building project, for a pre-tax profit of $8.7 million upon completion.

The total cost is $34.9 million, and the total sale proceeds is $43 million. This is our actual projected NOI for the project, but follows CMHC rules. The 3.85% capitalization rate is from a $44.3 million valuation less selling cost sale proceeds minus total cost. This results in a profit of $8.7 million—essentially an 87% IRR for the project if it is sold upon stabilization and completion. The return on cost of about 25% with development yield at 4.9% is very healthy.

This is another view of the same development.

NOI at stabilization (full year 1)	1,705,127
NOI Dedicated to Loan Payment	(1,314,399)
Net Cash Flow Before Tax (full year 1)	390,728
Eligible CMHC Loan (at strict criteria)	33,214,212
Total Project Cost	34,904,043
Equity Remaining After Takeout Financing	(1,689,832)
Projected Equity Injection	1,900,000
Equity IRR - 5 Year	61.4%
Equity IRR - 7 Year	45.6%
Equity IRR - 10 Year	35.4%
Development Yield	4.9%
Total Development Costs per unit	279,232
Total Development Costs per sqft	542
Value of Building if Sold in Year 10	49,876,608
Value per Unit at Sale in Year 10	399,013
Value per sqft at Sale in Year 10	775

Figure 3.21 - Affordable Return on Investment - Alt View

The net cash flow is $390,728, which equates to about 23% return on the net remaining equity. There is $1.7 million in the project, and the project in IRR numbers is pretty healthy for all three holding periods: five, seven, and 10 years. The best outcome is to sell it upon completion. In terms of investments and return, we consider it to be a doable project. Note that, generally, affordable housing requires a lot of work upfront compared to conventional rental projects.

Conventional Housing Building

These are highlights from the same financial model and building, but built as a conventional building.

UNIT TYPE	SQFT	# OF UNITS	% TOTAL	MONTHLY $	ANNUAL $	$/SQFT
Studio	410	40	32%	1,538	18,450	3.75
1-bedroom	535	70	56%	2,006	24,075	3.75
2-bedroom	700	15	12%	2,625	31,500	3.75
TOTAL	64,350	125	100%	241,313	2,895,750	3.75
AVERAGE	515	Res Only		1,931	23,166	3.75

OTHER INCOME				MONTHLY $	ANNUAL $
Laundry	–			–	–
Parking Revenue	100 STALLS	x	$100	10,000	120,000
TOTAL OTHER INCOME				10,000	120,000

			MONTHLY $	ANNUAL $
Total Potential Gross Revenue			251,313	3,015,750
Less: Vacancy and Collection Loss	@	3.0%	7,539	90,473
EFFECTIVE GROSS INCOME			243,773	2,925,278

Figure 3.22 - Development Mix and Revenue - Conventional

We'll assume regular uncontrolled rents at approximately $3.75 per square foot per month—this is pretty reasonable in today's market for this configuration. Note that 100 parking stalls are required, which is minimal as compared to 125 units but subject to certain relaxation. You can probably get away with it, otherwise you'll need all 125. However, with parking ratios being reduced, $100 per month is not enough to recover building the parking space.

Vacancy and collection loss is 3%—which does not apply for the affordable version.

OPERATING EXPENSES	PER UNIT	%	PER SQFT	MONTHLY	ANNUAL $
Property Taxes	3,500	49%	6.80	36,458	437,500
Insurance	250	4%	0.49	2,604	31,250
Repair & Maintenance	750	11%	1.46	7,813	93,750
Utilities	900	13%	1.75	9,375	112,500
Staff (Ops & Maint)	800	11%	1.55	8,333	100,000
Gen Admin & Marketing	100	1%	0.19	1,042	12,500
Management Fee 3.5%	819	12%	1.59	8,532	102,385
TOTAL EXPENSES	7,119	100%	13.83	74,157	889,885

Figure 3.23 - Operating Expenses - Conventional

The operating expenses are about 30% of the revenue. (Do not assume that 30% is the regular operating expense percentage; it just happens to be in this case.) The staffing costs are a bit higher as well.

Below are the development costs for a conventional building. We have kept the land costs the same to highlight the key variances from an affordable building.

CONSTRUCTION	CMHC STANDARD (MARKET RENTAL)	PER UNIT	PER SQFT	%
Land	6,435,000	51,480	100	14.4%
Construction	26,254,800	312,998	408	58.7%
Professional Fees	1,193,400	9,547	19	2.7%
Development Management	686,587	5,493	11	1.5%
Permits and Approvals	6,084,290	48,674	95	13.6%
Marketing and Leasing	796,884	6,375	12	1.8%
Financing and Interest	2,093,763	34,838	33	4.7%
HST (Self Supply)	2,260,945	18,088	35	5.1%
Operating Income During Lease-Up	(1,115,987)	(8,928)	(17)	-2.5%
TOTAL DEVELOPMENT COSTS	44,689,682	357,517	694	100%

Figure 3.24 - Development Costs - Conventional

Construction costs go up due to parking changes and added amenities—$408 per square foot compared to $357 for the affordable version. Also, parking permits and approvals are $95 per square foot as compared to lower, or probably no, cost. The total development cost comes to $694 compared to $542—this is about 29% more.

NOI at stabilization	2,159,975
Capitalization Rate	4.00%
Valuation @ $2.67 per sqft avg rent	53,999,378
Less: Selling Costs	(809,991)
Sales Proceeds	53,189,387
Total Cost	44,689,682
Profit Before Taxes if Sold at Stabilization	8,499,705
Return on cost	19.0%
Development Yield	4.8%
IRR upon stabilization if sold	19.5%
IRR 10-Year	20.4%
Construction Costs per unit	357,517
Construction Costs per sqft	694
Value per unit at Stabilization	431,995
Value per sqft at Stabilization	839

Figure 3.25 - Return on Investment - Conventional

Return on investment at stabilization is $2.159 million. We have used a 4% cap rate for a valuation of about $54 million less selling cost proceeds—total costs $44 million.

Before tax profit, if sold at stabilization, is $8.5 million, which is about 19% return on cost, based on the investor return requirements. This project achieves a good development yield of 4.8%. IRR upon stabilization is 19.5%.

If the developer wants to hold the project post completion, the takeout financing helps to retrieve the entire invested capital.

NOI at stabilization (full year 1)	2,159,975
NOI Dedicated to Loan Payment	(1,768,522)
Net Cash Flow Before Tax (full year 1)	391,453
Eligible CMHC Loan (at strict criteria)	44,689,682
Total Project Cost	44,689,682
Equity Remaining After Takeout Financing	-
Projected Equity Injection	11,000,000
Equity IRR - If Sold Upon Stabilization	19.0%
Equity IRR - 5 Year	21.4%
Equity IRR - 7 Year	21.4%
Equity IRR - 10 Year	20.4%
Development Yield	4.8%
Total Development Costs per unit	357,517
Total Development Costs per sqft	694
Value of Building if Sold in Year 10	60,812,070
Value per Unit at Sale in Year 10	486,497
Value per sqft at Sale in Year 10	945

Figure 3.26 - Return On Investment - Conventional - Alt View

As shown, there is a $391,453 net cash flow with projected equity at $11 million based on a 25% equity of the total cost. The IRR numbers are good for the different periods. Five-year plus holding period yields the highest IRR.

Key Differences

The key differences between affordable and conventional, based on our experience.

	AFFORDABLE	CONVENTIONAL
Rent	Controlled	Market
Property Tax	No	Applies
Parking Cost	Low Parking #s Reduce Cost	Min. Parking Cost Applies
Amenities Cost	Low Amenities, Low Cost	Certain Min. Amenities are a Must
Development Charges	No	Applies
Park Dedication Fee	No	Can be a Significant Cost
Financing	Generous Loan Terms	Market
Sale Upon Completion	Can Be Sold with Profit	Can Be Sold with Profit
Play	Procedurally More Complex Strings Attached You Can Hold for Long Term	Merchant Builder Model No or Low Strings Attached You Can Hold for Long Term
Cap Rate	Market	Market
Equity Requirement	Low	Conventional
EQUITY RETURNS ON THE MODEL PRESENTED		
Equity Investment	1,900,000	11,000,000
Profit if Sold on Completion	8,720,622	8,499,705
Equity Multiplier	5.59	1.77

Figure 3.27 - Key Differences

Rent is controlled in affordable housing while market rent applies for conventional housing. Property taxes don't apply to affordable housing and parking costs are lower, reducing development costs. Market apartments require more amenities—much fewer are required for affordable housing. Toronto does have a minimum amenity area requirement. But market amenity areas could be of higher quality, if not necessarily larger.

Development charges, property taxes, cash-in-lieu, Section 37, etc., can be waived in affordable, but the maximum rent is also substantially reduced and controlled—this does not apply to conventional. Park and dedication fees can be waived in affordable, but will be a significant cost in conventional development. For financing, you get generous long terms for affordable, while for conventional you get market—other than some CMHC programs. Sale upon completion: both can be sold for profit.

In terms of play, affordable is procedurally more complex with strings attached, but you can hold it for the long term as well. For conventional, the play is the merchant builder model, with no or few strings attached. You can also hold for the longer term.

Conventional cap rate should be equal or lower than affordable as there is more potential for the rent to increase. Equity requirement is low in affordable (provided that the rents are not compressed by city restrictions—on top of CMHC's—to the point that equity is closer to 25%). For conventional, you pay conventional equities—about 25% is a reasonable assumption.

Overall, a much higher equity multiplier for affordable is possible—5.59. The catch is, you must go through hoops of bureaucratic channels with affordable housing as compared to conventional development.

Tips for Successful CMHC Rental Construction Financing Initiative (RCFi)

These tips come from our experience with projects successfully funded through the RCFi.

1. Before Applying

It's very important to understand that affordable housing may not be a good fit for all rental projects.

- Zoning to be in place. SPA can be undergoing
- Rent 10% below market, as determined by an appraiser
- Process takes an average of 6 months

RATIO RENT TO BUDGET

- ✓ High rent locations can sustain high-rise developments with underground parking and higher land values
- ✓ Low- to mid-rent locations can sustain wood-frame or light gauge steel mid-rise developments with surface parking and moderate land value
- ✓ In-fill apartment complexes can sustain high-rise developments with shared use of existing parking. Equity can be mainly land

CASH EQUITY

- ✓ Can be minimized by maximizing loan amount and rent

Figure 3.28 - Before Applying Tips

CMHC expects shovel-ready sites with zoning in place. The Site Plan Agreement (SPA) can be undergoing at the time of your application. The application usually takes six months—something to consider in your project timeline.

The rent must always be 10% below market as determined by an appraiser. You are not bound by the stats that CMHC produces every year. You get an appraisal report that informs the developer and CMHC what the rents are—the specific rents that apply. The more bullish the report is from the appraiser, the higher the rents will be because they are discounted by 10%.

As for location of the project, it's important to understand that the rent and site zoning will determine what potential projects you can consider. We call it the ratio between rents to budget: when location rents are high, let's call it $4 per square foot, there's more flexibility to build a building that could be a high-rise. It may be a concrete building with underground parking. In cases where your rent is much lower, let's call it mid to low rent, a developer will not be able to build a high-rise, but it may work for mid-rise, wood-constructed buildings of two to four storeys when combined with surface parking to reduce your budget and moderate land values.

An exception to this (a very interesting case), is that there are many properties available throughout the province that are infill apartment complexes—tower apartment complex with excess land (because that was the way they were designed in the '60s and '70s). Landowners have an opportunity to convert that excess land into a new building.

For instance, some of the amenities or parking space may not be fully utilized. A new building can take advantage of that and may not need the full construction of a new parking structure.

Also, the land is excess—zero cost to the development. It's very important to understand that the program is highly leveraged. You can get 95% of your total budget in the form of a loan. However, to minimize your cash equity, you will have to maximize your loan and try to accomplish the highest rents possible—it's a balancing act.

2. Online Application

Let's get into the program itself.

- Social outcome grid scores projects out of a total of 25 points
- Financial Viability
  - Project must be financially viable
  - Developer must have capability to carry the project without additional funding
  - Minimum debt coverage ratio requirements of 1.1x for the residential portion
- Affordability
- Energy Efficiency - At least 15% below the 2015 National Energy Code for building
- Accessibility - At least 10% of the units must meet or exceed accessibility standards

TIPS

✓ Projects need to hit a minimum of 18/25 points to succeed in being approved

✓ Minimum qualification points vary by region and current program competition

✓ Achieve additional points by having discounts in place for more than the prescribed (Not recommended to have deeper discounts on the rental rates)

✓ THE KEY to score the highest is by maximizing the affordability component as that is truly what CMHC cares about

Figure 3.29 - Online Application Tips

CMHC is looking for experience. If a developer doesn't have that experience or has not done something similar before, they should associate with someone or an organization that has. This way, at least for their first project, they have a better chance of approval.

Approval is based on a social outcome grid (which has 25 points). A developer must try to score as high as possible since they're competing with all other developers or applicants in the same area. The more points, the greater the chance of success.

The project must be financially viable. The developer must be capable of carrying the project; associate with a partner who can fill all the weak areas.

The developer is responsible for the loan during construction; the loan is recourse during that period.

Affordability is probably the most important element of this grid; it's weighted very heavily by CMHC. In order to achieve this, the project must be viable at 90% of market rents. Note that not every unit has to be discounted by 10%. The best located units can be set as market rent. The poorly located units, or those unappealing in some way, can be reduced below the 90%. On average, CMHC is looking for a 90% rent compared to market. Also, note that 20% of the units must be below 30% of the median household income.

The secret, or the advantage, is that CMHC does not require that you have a mix of units to accomplish this. You can have the smallest unit with the lowest rent and still be below the mark. For example, if you were to build in Ottawa, the 30% median household income is over $2,500 per month. If you take your small units, basically your bachelors, that rent in that market around $1,100, or if you don't have enough bachelors, you can continue with your one-bedroom units that rent around $1,500. This will be good enough for you to qualify for that 20% of units criteria.

Because it's a federal project program, the building must be energy efficient—15% below the 2015 national energy code. Find a consultant that will work on this with the architect and mechanical engineer to make sure that the building achieves those energy efficiency levels.

Accessibility is very important. At least 10% of the units have to meet or exceed the accessibility standard. They may cost a little bit more to build, but at the end of the day lease-up will be easy and quick.

Some Tips

You must maximize your points. A good rule of thumb is to achieve 18 points of the 25. However, this may vary. 18 points may not be sufficient in some markets, but enough in others. Remember, a developer is in competition with other developers in any given market. Toronto is highly competitive, likely needing more than 18 points.

To achieve a very high point score, a developer will have to go beyond the minimum CMHC requirements. For example, if CMHC asks for a 10-year term for affordability, a developer may go to an 11-year term or even longer. In the 11th year, they will be able to increase the rent by whatever the province allows. Adding an extra year (or years) of rent gets more points. You can also add a few more accessible rental units. Transit, or location in relation to transit, also gets more points. Getting government supports or a fast-track approval process from the municipality will give you extra points. However, government support may be tied to rental rates below 90%.

Things that are not recommended: discounting rent as well as lowering energy efficiency. The reason: 1) discounting rent (building at 85% rather than 90% of market) hurts the potential loan amount to be received; 2) the reason for not lowering energy efficiency: it will likely increase the budget for energy, offsetting any potential gain.

3. Prescreening

CMHC specialists are allocated by region. Contact the person that is in your region.

TIPS

- CMHC prescreens all applications, reviews for eligibility and completion, and gathers additional information, if required
  - ✓ Be in frequent contact with your CMHC specialist
  - ✓ If application is denied, find out why, make modifications, and reapply

Figure 3.30 - Prescreening Tips

As a developer, the CMHC contact person will want to know who you are, what you have built, what your proposed project is, and what market needs your project is fulfilling. When your application comes to them, it is vital they can relate that application or company name to someone specific, and to get the story behind the project to help them understand the strength of the group that is putting the application together.

CMHC will take some time to review an application and may come back for information before deciding if you qualify for the program.

4. Prioritization

Where does a developer fit in?

TIPS

- Projects are either approved and selected for underwriting, rejected, or kept on hold
  - ✓ Exceed the mandatory minimum requirements for financial viability, affordability, energy efficiency, and accessibility
  - ✓ Project to address a need for supply in the market

Figure 3.31 - Prioritization Tips

If approved, the CMHC will formally contact you by letter. If not, contact the CMHC specialist you have developed a relationship with and find out why. What in the application needs to be changed for approval? After changes are made, you can try again.

Don't give up. We're saying this, not because it's a slogan that everybody says, but because many first projects were rejected (sometimes twice). Once the right changes were made, those same projects were accepted.

5. Underwriting

The underwriter will ask for an endless number of documents. They will complete the full analysis of the developer's strengths and the project. Then they refer it and recommend it to CMHC.

TIPS

- Applications are subject to approval based on the underwriting assessment of the borrower, the property, and the market
- A third party underwrites for the program and acts for CMHC
- A large amount of studies must to be submitted, including Cost Consultants Reports
    - ✓ Ask for Studies RFP during the prescreening period
    - ✓ Work with a management consultant or a broker experienced with RCFi to maximize your points prior to submission and protect your interest

Figure 3.32 - Underwriting Tips

Note that CMHC has hired a third-party underwriter. In this case, it's a company by the name of CMLS. CMLS is the entity that will deal with the developer, and ensure the project is viable and has checked all the right boxes. It will then determine the loan amount that the project can qualify for.

There is a huge list of CMLS requirements, similar to when you go to a bank for your first loan. At the moment, you submit your online application, then go back and see what is on that list. The list is available on the CMHC website along with other studies needed specific to your site.

Ask consultants for a request for proposal (RFP). You don't have to approve or decide who will carry the studies, but at least when you need them, you can commission them and submitted to CMLS more quickly.

It is important to always have somebody with experience to help with this and to connect with the underwriter. You will be able to reinforce some points that may seem weak. You can negotiate with them about some position decisions or challenge with supportive documentation.

6. Approval and Letter of Intent

From this point, the underwriter sends in their decision and documentation to the CMHC Credit Committee.

TIPS

Final review and approval decision by CMCH Credit Committee, followed by the issuance and execution of Letter of Intent (LOI)

- ✓ Get familiar with previous approved projects LOIs
- ✓ Make sure that you negotiate all conditions at the LOI stage
  → CMHC is less flexible at Loan Agreement Stage

Figure 3.33 - Approval and LOI Tips

Normally CMHC will follow the underwriter's advice. The committee approves most of the cases and the loan.

Make sure you negotiate all conditions at the Letter of Intent (LOI) stage. The LOI is a detailed document, usually around 15 to 16 pages, which forms the basis of the lending agreement. It's better to negotiate at this stage because CMHC is more flexible at the LOI stage than at the loan agreement stage.

7. Loan Agreement and Funding

Some points here may be negotiated at the LOI stage, above.

TIPS

AGREEMENTS

- These are long (60-90 pages). Borrower covers all legal costs
- Have expiration dates unilaterally extended by CMHC
- CMHC will not provide in its facility for Letters of Credit (LC) for municipal securities or potential trade Liens or Construction Loan Carveout / Operating Line.

ALL PROJECT OVERRUNS ARE 100% PAID BY BORROWER

- ✓ Time the execution of the agreement with your SPA and Building Permit
- ✓ Provide wording in the agreement that:
  - First advance can be received before full SPA execution
  - Construction can start with a conditional building permit or commence order, rather than full building permit
  - Severance of parcels and correspondent security releases are allowed
  - LCs from other lenders can be secured as a 2nd mortgage
- ✓ Get an Operating Line from another lender secured by another asset. CMHC will not allow to secure it against the project lands

Figure 3.34 - Agreement and Funding Tips

The agreements themselves are usually quite long (60 to 90 pages). The developer and their legal counsel will have to deal with CMHC's outside law firm for the agreement.

The borrower covers all the legal costs. These costs are usually added to the project budget. After the loan agreement is signed and executed, you have only six months for the first draw.

Time the execution of the agreement with the SPA and building permit before you begin construction—before the end of the six months allowed before the first draw. If the six-month period ends, renewal is possible—usually renewed unilaterally by CMHC.

Unlike other lenders, CMHC will not include in its facility letters of credit to pay for municipal securities or a letter of credit that you arrange with your other lenders to cover potential trade liens. Nor will it arrange or allow to have a construction loan carved out of operating lines. Meaning, you will have to get funds from a third party. Also, CMHC, like any other lender, will tell you that 100% of any overrun must come from equity. If you get into this situation with other lenders, you may have the lender cover part of that overrun—however, we have not seen any CMHC loan where it is flexible on this.

Tips

Time your SPA and your building permit so everything is finalized within those six months of signing the lending agreement. The lending agreement must provide some wording to this effect. In case something does not go as per plan, the first advance can be received before you have the SPA executed. Also, the construction can start with a conditional building permit or commencement work order because one of the triggers for the first draw is the beginning of construction.

The trigger for construction to start, from CMHC's point of view, is that you have a permit. All of this must tie together and be as flexible as possible.

In cases where you have to sever parcels for the property (for instance, if you have an existing building and have to sever the land where the new building is being built), include in the agreement the right to sever during construction. Make sure that in the agreement the securities and company that owned the existing buildings are released after the severance.

As CMHC will not include a Letter of Credit (LC) in its facility, request that the agreement allow other lenders to place a second mortgage on the property to secure the LC.

It's best if all the tips mentioned here are included in the LOI.

Conclusion

When this process is done properly and can be financed by this type of initiative, it is, so far, the best available financial opportunity or initiative for purpose-built rentals in Canada, so long as you follow all these steps carefully.

Creating a Team for the Less Experienced

CMHC requires five years worth of housing experience. Many developers haven't built affordable housing before and don't have that experience. So, how do you create a team that does?

A developer must have a strong, experienced general contractor in place, and must prove that they have built projects on time and on budget. If you can find a partner with this experience, it enhances the probability of getting approvals in place. You are essentially competing against all the other applicants. Those who have the strongest support and meet the metrics will get their projects approved.

Forming a competent, experienced team, at least for the first few projects, greatly increases your ability to get approved.

Class-A Budget

CMHC requires a Class-A budget to be produced. How, and from whom, can you get this done?

You'll likely hire a cost consultant and/or quantity surveyor for this. The drawings must be advanced enough, and have the right details, to be Class A. This is done when the drawings are 70% to 80% advanced, usually after your application for building permits is submitted.

4

Working with Municipalities and Stakeholders

In building affordable housing, a developer is working with the municipality and other stakeholders in a much more intimate way than if they were building a luxury apartment building as a private developer. It is an additional part of the business that developers already are familiar with, but taken to a much higher level.

1. Basic Deal

As a developer, you will be providing affordable housing at rental rates set as a function of the CMHC Average Market Rent (AMR).

However, the Toronto Housing Secretariat has proposed a new definition of affordable rent, which has not been ratified yet, but likely will be shortly.

What may change? As an example, for a two-bedroom apartment, its AMR was $1,661 per month, and now may be a range of $929 to $1,661. This is going to change some of your pro forma going forward.

What do you get in return for building affordable housing? Usually, you get reduced waivers and capital grants that make up for your loss in net operating income.

The Basic Deal – Weston Artscape

Figure 4.1 - Weston Artscape

We believe there is room for creativity in this process. Many times, you may not have the initial capital to build a project or to build the full aspects of the project. Partnering with a nonprofit or building affordable into your pro forma will help you build the project. Going forward, more projects will have affordable housing components to them. The Weston Artscape is a classic example of a partnership between government and the private sector.

Weston Artscape

The Weston neighbourhood has historically had a lot of funding and/or economic development. It was identified as one of the city's 31 Neighbourhood Improvement Areas—areas with high rates of unemployment and lacking affordable housing.

In this case, there was a surplus of above-surface parking area owned by the Toronto Parking Authority. The City of Toronto, with the Rockport Group as the developer, the Toronto Parking Authority, and Artscape (a nonprofit group), came together and proposed a solution for the city. They realized they could take this surplus land to build affordable housing for the area.

The cost would come to about $10 million plus another $3 million in ongoing costs. The group came up with an interesting structure on how to pay for this project. The developer guaranteed the capital cost of the project, and made sure that there were no cost increases that the city would bear. The developer also provided a letter of credit as security.

In return, funding was made available through a number of ways, including grants and waivers of certain development charges (including waiver of the Section 37 monies that the developer would normally pay). In the end, they came up with a nice project that had 200 square feet of art space, 370 apartment units, six affordable units, and about 26 affordable live-work units where artists can live and showcase their projects and talents— basically, improving the community as a whole. This also created 940 jobs in the area.

Know Who Will Live There

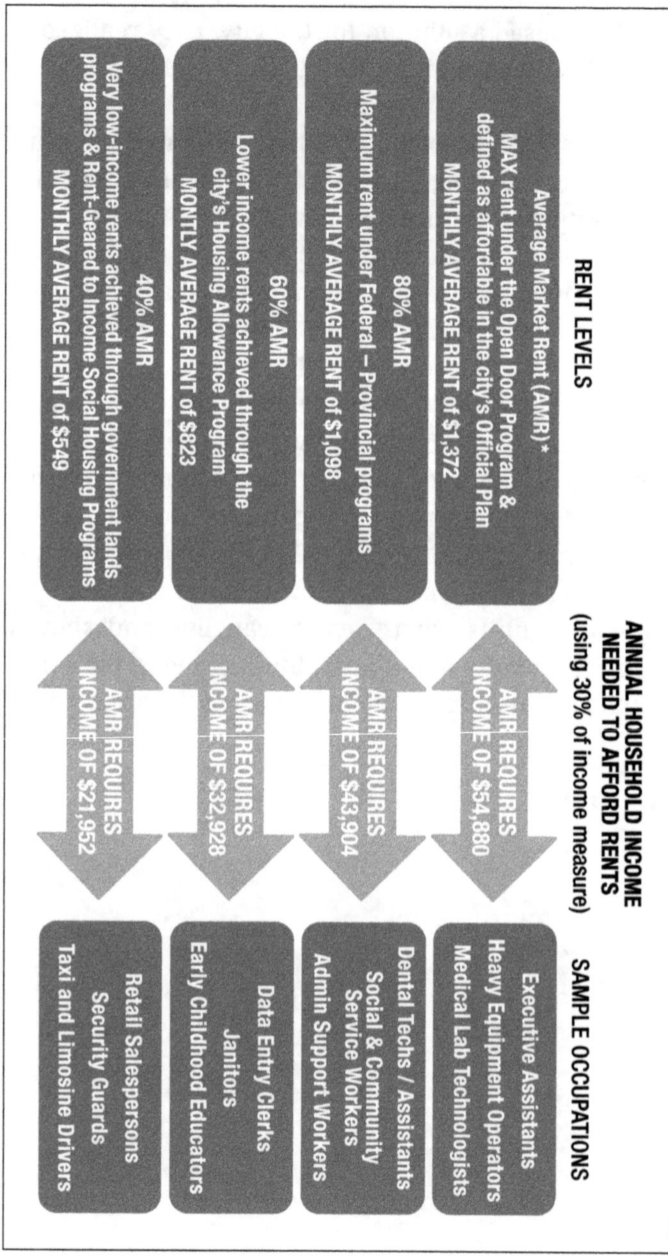

Figure 4.2 - The Basic Deal

From the developer's point of view, they must understand affordable housing and who they are trying to house. So, who are the rental candidates?

Depending on the program, the criteria may change. At the lowest range, you get a 40% AMR. These are individuals who are paying a monthly average rent of $549. This information is based on 2019 numbers and includes individuals whose annual gross income is just under $22,000, such as security guards, taxi drivers, and retail salespersons.

At the highest, 100% AMR, are individuals making incomes around $55,000 and paying a monthly average rent of about $1,400. These are executive assistants, heavy equipment operators, and medical laboratory technologists.

The Stakeholders

Most of a developer's interactions will be with public servants. Usually, many departments will be responsible for making decisions: the finance department, the housing department, and the planning department. They all have different objectives that you must strive to meet. They have a mandate, and municipalities have mandates to be more conservative.

There is also more reporting and more bureaucratic red tape than market rental. Decision-making is quite difficult because there is no individual decision-maker, especially at the municipal level—usually many people are involved.

Local politicians are also key individuals. Tip: try to get city councillors on your side. They can be your greatest champion, or they can hold up your project. A single city councillor, if not on your side, can delay a project for years. We have seen this happen. They simply raise an objection in city council, and the other councillors generally don't go against their fellow councillors, especially if the project is in their ward.

With local residents, you'll find that there are two sides—those in favour, and those who oppose—many times due to NIMBYism or the stigma surrounding affordable housing. You must engage both sides early on. Get them involved in the process and decision-making as much as possible. (Nothing is better than going to city council and having residents there to advocate on your behalf.)

Cities usually have a deputation policy. It allows members of the public and citizens to have their say—usually about five minutes on a topic. If you have a project that needs city council approval, and have about five to 10 residents come in and say how your project is the greatest thing since sliced bread, politicians will listen, and may be more likely to approve the project.

2. Learn to Speak Housing

Public servants' main role is to fulfil public policy objectives. They must provide safe, secure housing for all.

- Public servants' aim is to fulfil a public policy objective
  → Safe, secure housing for all
- Respect their role and align your development with that goal
  → Consider Weston - City's support gained through alignment with:
    ✓ New Rentak at the *UP/GO Weston Transit Node*
    ✓ New affordable rentals for artists
    ✓ Nonprofit partner
    ✓ Accessible units
    ✓ New community facility
    ✓ Cool common space & a home for *Weston Farmers Market*
    ✓ Creative reuse of a "not-so-pretty" building

Figure 4.3 - Speak Housing

Municipalities are risk-averse organizations. Present proposals that reduce their risk. Often, this is in the form of guarantees. Rockport, as part of its project with Artscape, guaranteed any excess construction cost. If you can reduce the risk for government, it's more likely that you will have your project approved.

Governments also have different types of programs. If you are trying to build a housing project and the priority for the government is transport, you're not going to get the visibility unless you somehow tie it to transportation. You must identify what programs are the current favourites and try to tie your project to those programs.

The Artscape project aligned itself with the transit nodes. It also aligned itself with a nonprofit partner. Any time you partner with nonprofits, provide accessible units or a community facility to make the whole area look better. Politicians will take notice.

At the Federal Level

The National Housing Strategy Act defines Canada's housing policy. This act recognizes that there is a fundamental right to adequate housing. It recognizes that housing is essential to the inherent dignity and well-being of the person. It advocates for improved housing outcomes and furthers the progressive realization of the right to adequate housing.

- *National Housing Strategy Act:* Housing Policy of Canada
    - a) recognize that the right to adequate housing is a fundemental human right affirmed in international law
    - b) recognize that housing is essential to the inherent dignity and well-being of the person and to building sustainable and inclusive communities
    - c) support improved housing outcomes for the people of Canada
    - d) further the progressive realization of the right to adequate housing as recognized in the *International Covenant on Economic, Social and Cultural Rights*
- These are obligations of the *Government of Canada*, not an enforceable individual right to access housing
- When participating in federal programming, you are a delivery mechanism for this policy objective
- Most home builders are natural allies of this expression of the right to adequate housing

Figure 4.4 - Housing Rights

All of this is nice to say, but what does it mean? It does not mean that individuals without housing can sue the government, and say, "OK, I need housing based on these principles." However, it is an obligation for the Government of Canada to provide housing. Now, why would the Government of Canada advocate for these fundamental rights? Why would it put more obligations on themselves?

Some of us would believe that it is a fundamental human right. But there is an economic aspect to this. By providing more affordable housing, you are actually reducing overall cost to government. Multiple studies have proven that health-care costs drop, and the justice system sees reduced expenses, especially in disadvantaged areas. Additionally, jobs are created in the process.

Overall, government investments create a higher return, especially when you consider all the outcomes. So, when you, as a developer, participate in federal incentive programs, you are a delivery mechanism for its policy objectives, thus becoming an ally. The more housing you build, the more housing becomes available. There is synergy; a partnership between government and the private sector, especially in the development of housing.

3. Know the Criteria and the Process

Different programs have different criteria.

- QUALIFYING FOR AFFORDABLE HOUSING PROGRAMS CAN MEAN DIFFERENT THINGS
  - → *Rental Construction Financing Initiative* (RCFi) - CMHC
    - ✔ 10% below achievable rent
    - ✔ 20% of units must be at or below 30% of local median household income
    - ✔ Project must decrease energy use and GHG emissions (15% below the 2015 National Energy Code for Buildings)
  - → *Open Door – City of Toronto*
    - ✔ Average Market Rent
    - ✔ 50% of the gross floor area (GFA) must be affordable
- JUST BECAUSE YOU DO NOT QUALIFY FOR ONE, DOES NOT MEAN YOU SHOULD STOP LOOKING AT OTHER PROGRAMS

Figure 4.5 - Know the Criteria

In the Rental Construction Financing Initiative, a federal program under CMHC, you must meet 10% below achievable rent targets. Twenty percent of the units must be at, or below 30% of local medium household. There are also greenhouse emission gas reduction requirements to consider. Toronto's Open Door program has different requirements based on the AMR, the average market rent. 50% of the area must be affordable.

Note that, because you do not qualify for one program does not mean you should stop trying. There are plenty of programs out there. There are plenty of creative partnerships that you can be part of. Look around, you will likely be able to find something that meets your objectives.

The public sector is directed to use a public procurement process for certain projects. For some of the projects, it is an application process. For others, especially when you're partnering, you must use public procurement.

- Public Sector is directed to use public procurement processes for certain projects
  - → Understand these requirements of the bidding process
  - → There are exceptions to the procurement rules, but high threshold
    - ✓ *Direct Award* (i.e., sole source)
    - ✓ *Swiss Challenge System*
- Know who are the decision-makers
  - → Generally more than one in the public sector

Figure 4.6 - Know the Process

In the city of Toronto, the Toronto Community Housing revitalization projects are, in total, multi billion dollar projects. Ottawa is redeveloping areas as well. All of these go through the public procurement processes.

Public procurement does not guarantee that you are going to get the best value for your money. What it does guarantee is transparency—that's what the public sector is looking for. What this means is, it is often difficult for private sector developers who are used to approaching cities, or other partners, with proposals, to quickly make a deal. It is often difficult to approach the city with this process.

You must respect the city's processes—which involves a request for proposal process. There are very few exceptions. At times, you can do Direct Awards, but they are rarely used unless it is urgent or an emergency. For example, the Direct Award process has been used for some modular housing projects—due to the urgency of the situation.

There is also the Swiss Challenge System, which is an interesting process, but one not yet used. With this system, you propose a solution to the city—a proposal. The city takes the proposal, evaluates it, and, if it deems it viable, will ask if anyone else can do better. If no one comes forward, you get the contract. What often happens is your proposal is the only one presented; most bidders realize that the city wants to work with this proposal and will not challenge it.

4. The Contribution Agreement

The example we'll use is the Open Door Agreement.

THE CONTRIBUTION AGREEMENT

- ***THE CONTIBUTION AGREEMENT*** **IS AN AGREEMENT WITH THE MUNICIPALITY THAT SECURES AFFORDABLE HOUSING BENEFITS**
- **YOU SHOULD UNDERSTAND THAT:**
  - → It will carry security – charge on the land
  - → If you keep units affordable, the loan is forgiven
    - ✓ e.g. *City of Toronto*, reduces loans by 4% per year over 25 year period
- **NOT ALL FEES AND LEVIES ARE WAIVED**
  - → Among others, Catholic School DCs, public art, hydro are NOT waived
  - → *The Contribution Agreement* will set out all waived fees
    - ✓ e.g. property tax, development charges, planning application fees, building permit fees, TDSB levies, parkland dedication payment requirements
- **YOU WILL RECEIVE A LETTER TO BRING TO THE COUNTER TO PROVE THAT YOU DO NOT HAVE TO PAY FEES**
  - → DO NOT pay and then attempt to get money back. You won't be able to
- **WORRY ABOUT THE PAYMENT PROCESS**
  - → If funds are coming in lumps, you will need to borrow to pay trades
  - → Typically payments are made 30% at the beginning, 50% on structural framing, and 20% on First Occupancy
    - ✓ Payment based on milestone reporting
- **IT'S A LOAN, WITH REGISTERED SECURITY. POSTPONEMENT AGREEMENT WITH A LENDER IS NEEDED**
  - → Most Contribution Agreements permit this but require that a reasonable amount of equity remains available
- **MIND YOUR NEW RESPONSIBILITIES**
  - → You must income test tenants as they come in
  - → If the municipality has a wait-list for affordable, you must participate and 20% of Open Door units must be available for tenants on Housing Benefits
  - → There are reporting requirements
- **READ THE AGREEMENT!**
  - → Audit rights, privacy rights (MFIPPA), public acknowledgment requirements, etc. – unique to government contracts

Figure 4.7 - The Contribution Agreement

This is an agreement between the municipality and developer on securing of the affordable housing benefits. In this case, the city provides a forgivable loan—not a grant. It will carry security, usually in the form of a charge on the land. Sometimes it is a letter of credit. You can't really use a letter of credit over a 25-year period, which is often the term of these contracts. However, the letter of credit can be used in the shorter term—the construction period, for example—to meet the security requirements.

Generally, if you keep the units affordable over a certain period, the loan is forgiven. The typical time frame for an Open Door project is 25 years. Every year, 4% of your loan is forgiven. By year 25, your loan is totally forgiven.

As part of this deal, you get waivers on certain fees: property tax, development charges, and planning application fees are examples. However, not all fees are waived. Hydro is a good example, as are public art fees.

What you often get is a letter proving the fees are waived. When you go to contract and need to prove that you do not have to pay the fees, you provide this letter. If you are a part of these agreements and have the letter, do not pay the fees in the first place. If you do pay them, it is almost impossible to get them back—there's a lot of bureaucracy involved when trying to get those fees returned.

Also, know the payment process. You do not get the money in a lump sum ahead of time. Typically, you receive 30% in the beginning, 50% when structural framing is completed, and the remaining 20% when you have first occupancy. Payments are based on milestones, and you will have to provide reporting. It is a loan with registered security. With your lender, you will likely have to get a postponement agreement. Most lenders are understanding and receptive to such agreements.

You must mind your responsibilities. There are many strings attached to these agreements. The tenants that you have in affordable housing must meet certain defined income tests. Make certain you understand the new affordable rent criteria and ensure all tenants meet these requirements.

All this means extra administrative costs from your end. If the municipality has a waiting list, you must use that waiting list. As a result, you have very little say on who your tenants are going to be. But this is also a benefit to you because it lowers administrative costs. You are not really looking for tenants and there is no need to market the units—there is already a list of people willing to rent. There are numerous reporting requirements that must be met, including quarterly and annual reports.

Thoroughly read the agreement. Government contracts have provisions that you may not be familiar with. For example, audit rights. You must keep all the documents—the government, the municipality, the city have a right to audit your documents to ensure that you are meeting these requirements.

MFIPPA is the privacy legislation applicable to municipalities right across the province. What this means is, anyone paying a $5 fee can initiate a Freedom of Information request and get access to the contract that you have with the municipality—your contract with the municipality is not confidential. When you make a deal with the city, the Initial Contribution Agreement and your basic pro forma are going to be presented at city council and debated there—it's not going to be confidential in the first place.

Later, as you are administrating the contract, there will be ongoing requirements under MFIPPA. Some information that you may think is confidential may be released to the public. There are also public acknowledgments that you have received funding—it's a PR piece for both you and the products.

5. Outside Toronto

Outside of Toronto, the rules are pretty much the same.

- While the basic rules are the same, the benefits available come from two different levels of government
- The amount of money available in smaller communities can mean they undertake a funded project once every two or three years
  → *It's a very big deal and very visible*

Figure 4.8 - Outside Toronto

Understand that the benefits usually come from the provincial and/or the federal governments. The amount of money though, is less. There is less funding available outside of Toronto and there are fewer projects being undertaken. As a result, there is more scrutiny and strings attached to a project. Be wary of this—public money is being used, so there must be a certain level of scrutiny.

On the positive side, it gives you an opportunity to be in the good graces of the community for a long time if you do the project well and the outcomes are favourable.

6. The Future

A lot of what we've stated is inevitable. So what does that mean for the different sectors?

- Nonprofit housing providers are amalgamating, working through land trusts and becoming increasingly sophisticated
- They are, and will continue to, compete for land and buildings and will now be assisted by the *Rapid Housing Initiative*
- They have land and equity to bring to the table
- Consider partnering with a nonprofit

Figure 4.9 - Nonprofits

Nonprofits are becoming increasingly sophisticated. Many of the smaller nonprofits are amalgamating. We are assisting a number of amalgamations through land trusts and other structures, including creating substitution development, limited partnerships, and joint ventures. The public sector and nonprofits are using the same vehicles for development.

The nonprofit sector is also competing for land and buildings. With more funding available from different sectors, it is also competing with the private sector on purchasing land and buildings to be used for affordable housing.

There are different ways of partnering nonprofits and private sector entities. The classic one is just a simple land sale or transaction. But there have been joint ventures and other types of limited partnership arrangements created. Nonprofits now want to be genuine partners and share in the upside of deals, especially in hotter markets.

The difficulty for many nonprofits is that they have a low tolerance for any downside risk. It is their nature; it's the legislation. So there must be a carefully thought-out partnership between the two sides—this is possible and a lot of it is happening.

This is important because nonprofits have land. Some of them also have equity, and thus can bring that to your projects. Our main point is, when considering working with nonprofits, know that they bring a level of expertise to affordable housing that you may not have. They have relationships with municipalities that will help you get a project passed. In some ways, they might be your only way of getting certain deals done because certain deals are only available to nonprofits with partnerships.

Inclusionary Zoning

Inclusionary Zoning (IZ) is a provincial planning tool that enables municipalities to secure affordable housing in new developments. This new-to-Ontario policy intends to increase the supply of affordable housing for low- and moderate-income households, particularly in transit-connected locations.

The use of IZ is restricted to areas within a Protected Major Transit Station Area (PMTSA), a Development Permit System (DPS) area, or as ordered by the Minister. The Planning Act exempts IZ from developments which contain fewer than 10 residential units or are proposed by a nonprofit housing provider. The provincial Inclusionary Zoning regulation includes minimum transition provisions for the following applications made prior to the adoption of the IZ framework: an application(s) for an Official Plan amendment and/or a Zoning bylaw amendment (provided that an application has also been made for approval of a plan of subdivision or condominium approval); or application(s) for site-plan approval or a building permit.

THE FUTURE - Here Comes Inclusionary Zoning

- We can expect IZ to become a fixture over time as governments look for ways to increase affordable stock
  - → Prevalent in many other jurisdictions
- **APRIL 2018:** *O. Reg 232/18* of the *Planning Act* enacted
  - → Allowed municipalities to implement IZ
- **JUNE 2019:** *Bill 108, More Homes, More Choices Act, 2019* enacted
  - → Limited IZ to protected major transit station areas (PMTSA) + where development permit system required by MMAH
- **SEPT 2020:** City of Toronto Inclusionary Zoning Draft Official Plan Amendment and Zoning By-law Amendment
  - → IZ would apply to development in PMTSA located within strong or moderate market areas
  - → Units would remain affordable for 99 years
  - → At least 10% of the affordable rental GFA secured at rents based on 80% affordable rent definition
  - → 5-10% of total GFA of condominium development would be secured as affordable
  - → Report expected in September 2021

Figure 4.10 - Inclusionary Zones

The Planning Act requires that IZ frameworks be informed by assessment reports that analyze housing need and demand, as well as financial viability within a municipality, updated every five years. The Planning Act also stipulates that municipalities that wish to utilize this planning tool must update their Official Plans to include IZ policies that describe the following:

- The minimum development size for which IZ would be required
- The required number of units or gross floor area of affordable housing
- The range of housing types and sizes that would be authorized as affordable housing units
- The range of incomes for which units must be affordable
- How the price/rent is determined
- The conditions under which permission would be granted for off-site IZ dedication.

Given the restrictive geographic use of IZ, PMTSAs are where most IZ activity will occur (few areas of the province are designated as DPS areas), so it is imperative to understand what a PMTSA is and where they may be located.

Inclusionary Zoning is a way for including affordability as part of development and revitalization projects. It has been prevalent elsewhere in other jurisdictions for a long time. Most people are aware of the New York example where a certain percentage of buildings must be affordable housing. In 2018, the Planning Act was enacted to allow Inclusionary Zoning in Ontario. In 2019, it was modified slightly to pertain only to major transit station areas.

In Toronto, the Official Plan Amendment and Zoning By-law went to consultations in 2019. But there has been more ongoing consultation. A report delivered in November 2021 titled *Inclusionary Zoning Official Plan Amendment, Zoning-By-law Amendment and Draft Implementation Guidelines - Supplementary Report #2* should provide more context and clarity for what is going to happen in the future.

As anticipated, Inclusionary Zoning has been implemented for all apartment development going forward. The current draft bylaws require 99-year affordability in affordable housing buildings. The City of Toronto is going to require development in areas that have stronger moderate-market areas—it's not going to be in all areas. At least 10% of the affordable rental GFA must be secured at rates that are based on 8% of their new affordable rent definition, and 5% to 10% of the total GFA condominium development would be secured as affordable housing.

There is going to be more information coming out in the future. However, IZ is definitely on its way in. Developers must keep themselves updated on the latest developments and details.

Modular Housing

The Rapid Housing Initiative supports modular housing. It requires housing to be developed within 12 months. If a developer is able to develop housing in that time frame, modulars are a good way to go.

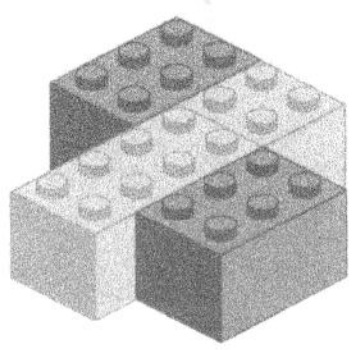

- *Rapid Housing Initiative* supports modular
- Recent *City of Toronto* rapid construction projects
  - → **Sole Source** agreement with *Horizon North Inc.* in April 2020 for 110 modular rental units
  - → **11 Macey Ave.** (56 units) opened in December 2020
    - 8 months after City Council approval
  - → **321 Dovercourt** (44 units) opened in January 2021
    - 9 months after City Council approval
- Future projects are to be via public procurement process

Figure 4.11 - The Future Is Modular

In April 2020, Toronto council approved 110 modular rental units of housing to Horizon North Inc. as a sole source contract (something they don't normally like doing). By December of that year, 56 units were developed at 11 Macey Avenue, and 44 units were developed at 321 Dovercourt Road—within nine months. The fact that the city expedited that development shows how serious it is about modular.

In our view, modular is here to stay. The city is now proposing more modular housing projects. What it has promised to do is move future projects through the public procurement processes.

The Federal Budget

There's more funding coming from the federal budget. The recent budget that was introduced had a number of initiatives.

THE FUTURE IS NOW – 2021 Federal Budget

- 2021 FEDERAL BUDGET
  - → To address COVID, Federal Government will invest and reallocate to speed up construction, repair or support of 35,000 affordable housing units
- AN ADDITIONAL $2.5 BILLION OVER 7 YEARS TO CMHC
  - → $1.5 billion for the *Rapid Housing Initiative* to add a minimum of 4,500 new affordable units
  - → $600 million to renew and expand the *Affordable Housing Innovation Fund* to create up to 12,700 more affordable housing units, including units for persons with accessibility challenges
  - → $315.4 million through the *Canada Housing Benefit*, to increase direct rent assistance for low-income women and children fleeing violence
  - → $118.2 million through the *Federal Community Housing Initiative* to support community housing providers that deliver long-term housing to vulnerable populations

Figure 4.12 - The 2021 Federal Budget

Because of the COVID-19 pandemic, there are going to be changes in many sectors. Housing is something that has been highlighted more of late. When COVID first hit, we were all told, "Go home, stay home, stay safe." That is very hard to do for people who don't have homes. In response, the government has put more emphasis on providing and expediting the investment into affordable housing units.

The recent budget has made $2.5 billion available to small and medium enterprises over seven years, which includes a $1.5 billion extension of the Rapid Housing Initiative to build 4,500 new affordable units. There are other initiatives, including $600 million for the Affordable Housing Innovation Funds—forgivable loans and other contributions to certain projects.

There are other projects. There has been the advancement of an additional $1.3 billion of previously announced funding. There's also funding for the homeless and for northern Canada. Going forward, there will be more funds from the federal government in support of affordable housing.

5

Developing a Business Plan to Build Affordable Housing

How do you approach the business from a philosophical standpoint, and how do you develop a long-term business plan to build affordable housing? There are seven steps to follow.

Note that we're making the assumption that you want to be in the development business, or are someone who helps developers achieve their goals.

We are also saying that, in an unstable business world, building affordable housing is quite stable and getting better. Though the label "affordable housing" may conjure an unflattering image, it is the wording currently in use. Practically, the housing will be occupied by income-generating individuals who deserve decent housing they can afford.

1. Consider Your Long-term Goals

In our view, the opportunities available in the affordable housing business are plentiful and sustainable. Housing affordability is one of the social and economic challenges of our time. It is a situation far different from the 1960s and '70s, where anyone could rent a decent apartment on a working man's wage spending about 20% or 30% of their income. That's not the case today. Both government and the private sector must address the current crisis.

There is bandwidth. It's not like we're going to build too much affordable housing. With significant demand available, lease-up will be very easy and vacancy rates will be low.

A trend is beginning. All levels of government are acutely aware of the shortage of affordable housing. This affects the economy negatively. They will, if they haven't already, put programs into place to provide incentives to build and streamline the process for developers and buyers.

All stakeholders realize that building affordable housing is a political and social winner. However, it's ultimately an economic winner for the developers who build it, the taxpayer who spends too much money on the wrong type of housing, and those in need of affordable housing.

There is a certain amount of effort that a developer must put in to learn the affordable housing business. It may not be worth their while to get up to speed for a single building. However, for those seeking a programmatic business, affordable housing is a great opportunity.

Though building affordable housing is trending positively on many levels, and bandwidth is available, it will not be a viable business if liquidity is absent. However, we do think there will be enough buyers and sellers. Historically, liquidity has not developed because municipalities had to be strongly encouraged to build affordable housing. When municipalities build something, they never trade it. The only time that affordable housing changed hands was when municipalities merged, government levels were adjusted, or there was a change from one social housing group to another. The private sector was never involved.

We believe that private sector involvement will create a viable affordable housing industry in an affordable, efficient, and scalable way. There is no limit to how much could happen if the right people get involved. Combined with the ESG movement, the path to the creation of more affordable housing is getting clearer and easier.

Other Considerations

Taxes

On disposition, the single largest cost will be the taxes paid. (These are not the owing municipal taxes.) When thinking about putting your assets in a trust for your children or your grandchildren, consider how taxes will affect the transfer.

Property Management

Property management is much more difficult when leasing market-rate apartments because all the risk occurs during lease-up; getting another 10 cents or 20 cents per square foot dramatically changes profits. With affordable housing, that square foot rent has already been capped.

The property management function now becomes more about customer service and the routine property management issues. There's no need for cutting edge, lease-up marketing and complex rent setting because, in theory, the building is going to fill as soon as the certificate of occupancy is issued, whether it be for the whole building or a temporary certificate of occupancy. The business of managing a fully affordable building is a lot simpler and greatly de-risked.

We believe that affordable housing is a wonderful opportunity right now, especially with historical low interest rates and the low terms that have been presented by CMHC affordable initiatives.

2. Determining a Site

Nothing happens until a site with affordable housing potential is found. Please refer to Chapter 2, "Where and What to Build" for a more detailed look at what and where to build.

Land Cost

Land cost will ultimately determine a large part of your construction performance. It is hopefully going to determine whether you have the ability to carry a percentage of your pro forma at below market rents, whether it's 90% or as low as 50% in some cases.

A good example: if a developer has been sitting on a piece of land for quite some time, or buys cheaply, that may be a viable site. Basically, a developer does not want to pay A+ condo prices for a piece of land, then try to make it work for affordable housing.

The Municipality

In many municipalities, you can't get affordable grants for all locations. Talk to your municipality to make sure that you understand where they provide affordable grants municipality wide or only in IZ or other designated zones.

Parking

If you have a quirky site with limited parking, it naturally lends itself to two things: student housing and affordable housing (because many municipalities will allow much more limited parking requirements for affordable housing).

Rent

Many CMHC grants and municipal grants rely on the percentage of the average market rent, based on income, to set rents. As an example, Woodbridge, Ont. has extremely high average market rents because they are based on incomes which are extremely high. In areas like this one, you can push the affordable rents (because 80% of the average market rent is very high). However, a site in Rexdale, Ont., where the average market rent is low because the average income is low, affordable rents are quite a bit lower.

Strategic Boundary Considerations

The average affordable rent changes dramatically from municipality to municipality. However, by building in a higher-rent municipality next door to one with lower rents, you can position a building for higher rents. If you can choose sites strategically like this, it is a huge advantage.

A similar strategy can be implemented with CMHC grants, which considers rents based on its own boundaries. If you are on the boundary between regions with different CMHC-set rents, choosing where to build can help your bottom line considerably. An example is Steeles Avenue in Toronto. One side of the street is in the city of Markham, the other side is in Toronto—they have different average affordable rents.

Infill Sites

Building new apartments on underused space in an existing site is also possible. Buildings constructed in the 1960s and '70s were built under very different regulation from those that currently exist. Space exists in those famous "towers in the parks" for new apartments.

This brings us to the situation where the land creates value. It becomes your long-term equity. There may even be a possibility to get some cash back at the beginning of the deal because you only need 5% to 10% equity, depending on the deal, to get long-term project financing.

In some situations, some apartment complexes have an existing parking structure that's only partially occupied, saving a developer money. By taking advantage of existing amenities and excess parking (or empty space), adding more rental space makes a lot of sense.

Many of these apartment complexes are currently in the hands of second- or third-generation owners who don't have the required development skills to build on the available space. Many are in the hands of REITs, public companies, or institutions, who also don't have development skills.

In this ESG world, we think that it's fair to say that public companies and institutions are under a certain amount of pressure to contribute to society. Affordable housing fits into that very nicely.

Though there is a learning curve and more red tape to deal with, affordable housing does not equate to lower profits.

3. Engage Early

When working with municipalities to build affordable housing, it's important to engage early with a clearly articulated plan. You must have land that is ready to build on, zoned properly and, hopefully, in early stage of SPA (Site Plan Agreement).

Municipalities view affordable housing projects completely differently from standard rental housing. From the beginning, a developer will be dealing with the local councillor as well as with planning staff—both ready to accelerate the project with flexibility.

For a developer, the planning documentation is long and confusing, requiring professional legal help. Often, there are multiple programs with overlapping boundary requirements.

Some councillors are very pro-affordable housing, and there are some who are very anti-affordable housing. It's good to understand this before you go into the municipality or into a council meeting. If you have a strong case and adhere to the program requirements, most municipalities will listen.

In the end, municipalities are going to try to tie any project to a current program. If you can tie it to that as well, you're more likely to be successful. Understand who the decision-makers are within a municipal environment. Usually, there's not a single decision-maker. With multiple decision-makers, the sooner you get involved, the better understanding you will have of the situation. You can build those relationships and develop internal champions who will help you advance your work.

4. Determine What to Build

Please refer to Chapter 2, "Where and What to Build" for a more detailed look at what to build.

The main point we want to get across is there are many different ways of structuring a project, whether it's 20% all the way to 60% (or more) affordable. When you start blending a building, it creates the issue of which units should be designated affordable.

Remember, all of your rents (of any type unit) are on a per-unit basis. This is going to impact your rent per square foot. Make them as small as possible, as long as they're adequately livable. If there are no limits on the unit types allowed, build bachelor units and one-bedroom units to improve your pro forma on a rent per square foot basis.

As for placement of the affordable units, do not segregate your building—don't put them all on one or two floors. Position them the same way as how you lease a market rental building—checkerboard fashion. There will always be some less desirable units on each floor that will only support lower rents because of positioning—proximity to elevators, garbage chutes, or stairwells. Those units become your affordable units.

If the building is 100% affordable, your amenity offering is going to be based on what the municipality or CMHC requires you to build. Please read and understand those requirements.

Think very carefully when planning finishes and features in a 100% affordable building. You are not likely going full top-of-the-line condo level. At the same time, you don't want to make it into something that looks too basic. The goal is to look modern, fresh, clean, and appealing. It will improve the reputation of the building. If you eventually sell the building, a good reputation is a definite plus.

When mixing affordable with rental, you can't skimp on amenities, finishes or features. The finishes and features should be fairly similar across all the units, especially from a costing standpoint. And the market-rent residents expect those nice amenities.

A few last points:

- With every partnership you enter into, think about how to get out of it
- We would lean toward recommending a building be built to minimum code—the goal is not to win an award, but to be profitable.

Building fully affordable buildings is viable business. Do not build something just to fit into a particular program. The goal is to become a programmatic affordable housing developer. For that to happen, there needs to be liquidity.

5. Determine Eligibility

Refer to Chapter 4, "Working with Municipalities and Stakeholders," for eligibility and requirements.

6. Complete a Detailed Financial Analysis

There are four factors to consider: financial viability, affordability, energy efficiency, and accessibility. The goal is to get as close to 25 points as possible—meaning you must get at least 18 points; and you have to excel in the affordability portion, which is what CMHC focuses on. The application has many steps: prescreening, prioritization, and finally underwriting. When it goes to underwriting, it is always important to be knowledgeable about the process, have the right team to work with, and be connected with CMHC before it goes to underwriting.

7. Determine Strategic Partnerships

We'll cover two types of partnerships: community stakeholders and nonprofit organizations.

With Community Stakeholders

In any community, there will be those in favour and those against new affordable housing. It is important to engage them early, get their input and involve them in the process. The last thing you need is to get in front of a municipality and have a group actively fighting against you.

With Nonprofits

What can nonprofits bring to a strategic partnership? In essence, they bring an understanding of the public sector, expertise in affordable housing, and a certain credibility to the municipality. All of which may help you get a project approved. Nonprofits are becoming increasingly sophisticated. They are interested in being involved in sharing the upside of a deal, but with a low tolerance for risks. That is something that you will have to manage.

Conclusion

There's no doubt that we need more affordable housing. The lack of coordination from different government levels has likely limited its development. However, the housing landscape is quickly evolving.

It is becoming apparent to all levels of government that the status quo cannot continue—the current approach is clearly inadequate. As a consequence, more effort and funding is now being brought forward to not only look at the problem, but to provide workable solutions; opening the door for creative and sustainable alternatives. As we explore this topic more as a community, and the municipalities, provinces, and federal government coordinate more comprehensively, we believe the opportunities for the private sector will grow quickly.

All levels of government have introduced incentives and have begun streamlining processes to make development faster. However, it comes with an increased bureaucratic burden on the developers. Governments often use public procurement processes. Though public procurement may not get the best value, it does provide the transparency required. Even with the increased workload and requirements, it is becoming apparent that the development of affordable housing is at least as viable as market development. Thus, there exists a path to liquidity and sustainability.

Whether you are building for the long term or the short term, the location is vital and location affects liquidity. Traditionally, buyers prefer major and secondary markets with proven potential. But secondary and tertiary markets are generating extraordinarily strong returns for apartment developers simply because the demand is so great and the competition is so low.

We also believe that funds will appear if the product becomes available. The environment is right, the market is right, and there is certainly no shortage of tenants. We predict a growing pool of buyers for affordable housing, but the buyers can't buy until the developers build, and developers don't want to build unless the buyers are there. With bureaucracy getting streamlined and more money becoming available, and more affordable housing stock being built and sold, there could be a real first-move advantage in developing affordable housing. Getting ahead of the business will create a real opportunity in the same way student housing initially developed.

Completing an affordable housing proposal to meet the governments' standards of scoring is not something many developers are familiar with when planning regular development projects. With different programs available, if a developer's pro forma doesn't fit into one program, it may fit well with others. There's always the opportunity to create a partnership to make a project viable.

We admit that many of the current programs are designed for nonprofits. The private sector can apply but they are not fully optimized to handle affordable housing's intricacies. Our role is to make this possible. We are going down this road together. We see this business becoming more institutionalized with professional affordable housing buyers and professional affordable housing builders. We must make this work because we need hundreds of thousands of apartments built to make up for what hasn't been built in the last 40 years.

Our commitment is to provide information to the private sector clearing the path to successfully building affordable housing in a programmatic way. Developers already have 90% of the expertise. Through our learning portal, our publications and our seminars, the remaining key 10% is available to any developer seeking to get an advantage in the housing market, be it affordable or market. We think that developers, and all stakeholders, will be surprised by how profitable affordable housing can be. And we think we know how to make this work for everyone.

Affordable housing is a growing field. By listening and adhering to what different government levels require and offer—which may be complex and onerous—developers can engage in a viable business. There may not be enough programs in place, and they may be somewhat complicated, but our goal as a company is to think ahead and prepare our clients for what surely will be coming down the pipeline.

Your Next Steps

1 Learn more about Derek Lobo and his Rock Advisors team at **RockAdvisorsInc.com** and be sure to plug into the industry news and key announcements. Here is what Derek and the team does:

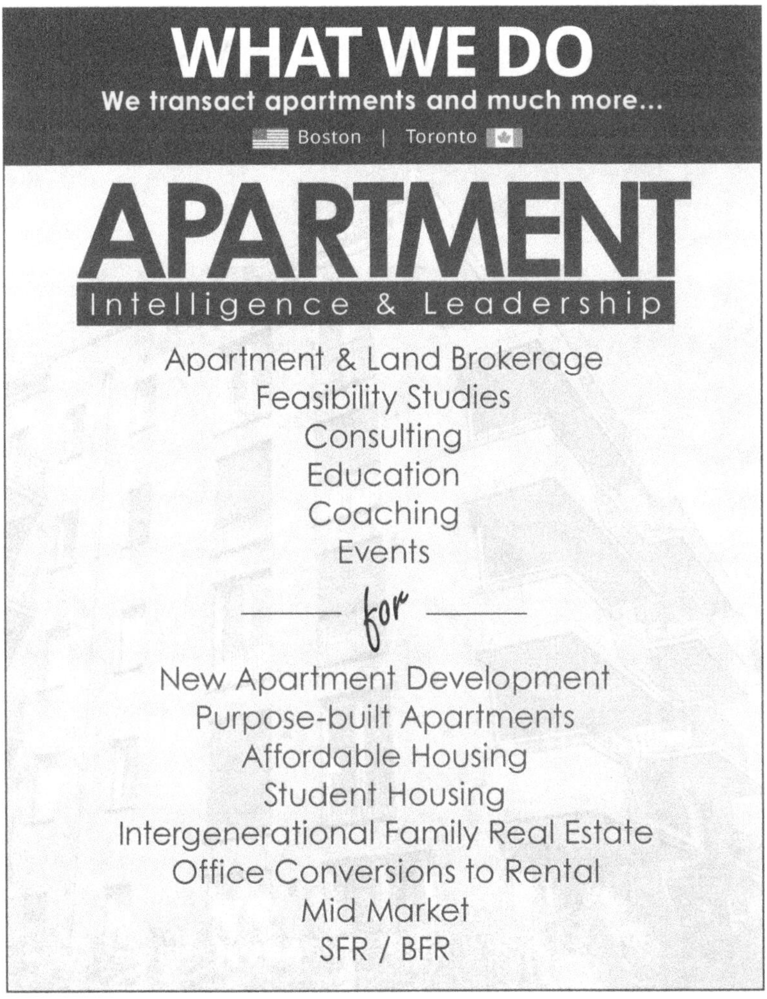

2 Connect with Derek's team to begin your journey of acquiring the content and connections to industry experts. **The Apartment Development FULL Service Experience™** is a value-adder for your complete project timeline.

CONTACT MY TEAM

Sales	**Director of Sales** 905.565.4404 Dave.Price@RockAdvisorsInc.com
Feasibility+ Research	**Business Development Manager** 905.565.4400 Christine.Lachapelle@RockAdvisorsInc.com
Apartment University™	**Director of Marketing** 905.565.4428 Rod.Schulhauser@RockAdvisorsInc.com

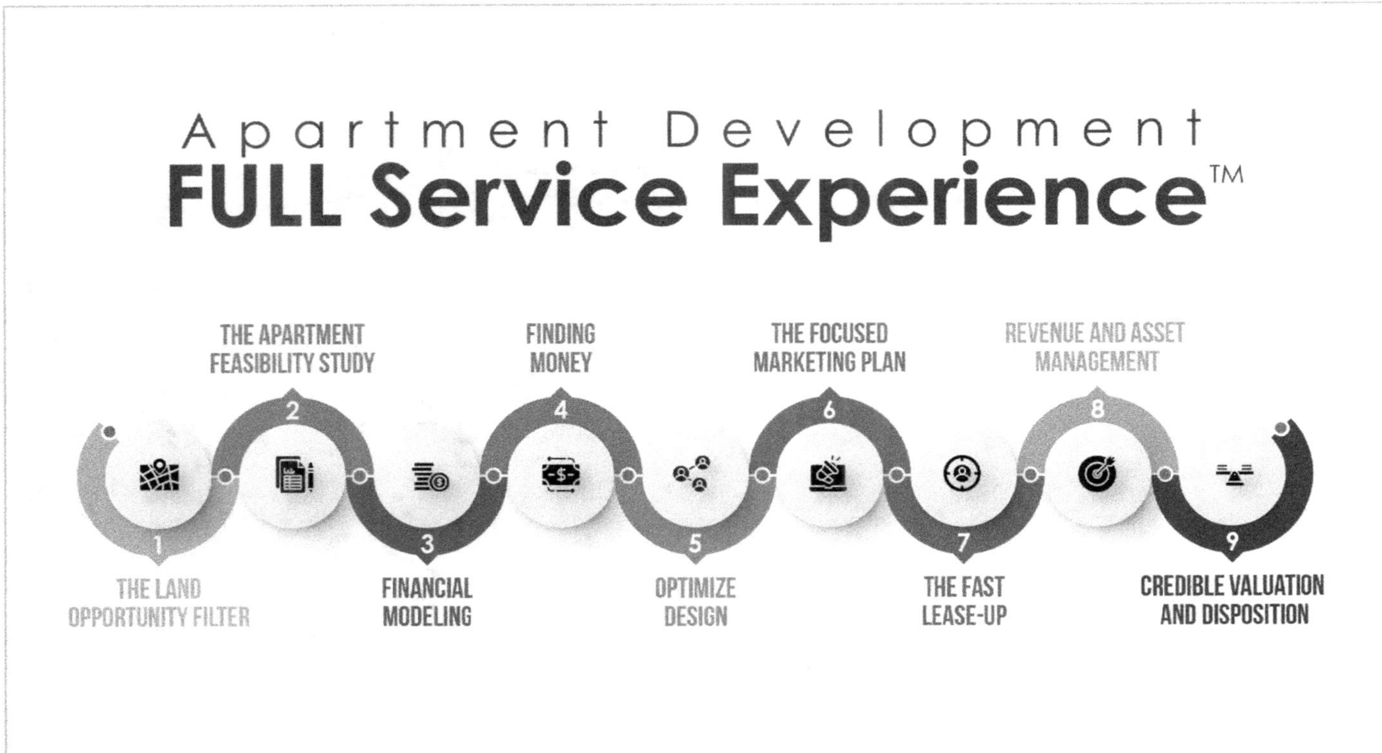
Apartment Development
FULL Service Experience™
1 THE LAND OPPORTUNITY FILTER
2 THE APARTMENT FEASIBILITY STUDY
3 FINANCIAL MODELING
4 FINDING MONEY
5 OPTIMIZE DESIGN
6 THE FOCUSED MARKETING PLAN
7 THE FAST LEASE-UP
8 REVENUE AND ASSET MANAGEMENT
9 CREDIBLE VALUATION AND DISPOSITION

3 The passion for arming apartment developers with the tools, relationships, knowledge, and coaching is the core focus! Derek has a mission...

About the Author

Derek Lobo is called the "Apartment Guru" because of his decades of speaking, writing, consulting, brokerage transactions, relationships, amortized knowledge, and industry wisdom. He is one of the most connected individuals in the apartment industry, living by his personal motto: Always stay in traffic!

As a student of new apartment construction, student housing, and affordable housing, Derek has established a sterling reputation and industry credibility as an expert advisor in these fields. To date, he has authored 18 books and is the visionary behind the ***Apartment University*** online learning portal.

Firmly established as a "thought leader," Derek's unwavering mission is to impact one of the world's greatest challenges—the lack of rental housing. He has leveraged his advisory expertise into his **Apartment Development FULL Service Experience**™ brokerage firm, which continues to serve landowners, financiers, developers, and apartment building owners.

Now in his fifth decade of business, Derek's desire is to become an "Apartment Collaborator." He is carrying out his vision by bringing together like-minded, talented individuals to work with him, solve business challenges inherent in the development industry, and create opportunities in the rental housing market.

Derek's keen insight and strategies have allowed him to broker some of the nation's largest and most complex real estate transactions. He is currently the Broker of Record and CEO of **SVN Rock Advisors Inc.**, Brokerage.

My Notes

My Notes

My Notes

My Notes

My Notes

My Notes

My Notes

www.ingramcontent.com/pod-product-compliance
Lightning Source LLC
LaVergne TN
LVHW020413220926
848484LV00017B/2556/J
* 9 7 8 1 7 7 7 3 6 4 8 6 1 *